The Law of Attraction

A Soulful Path

What you believe, you attract. What you feel, you become.

SHREE SHAMBAV

The Law of Attraction
A Soulful Path
Shree Shambav

Published by Shree Shambav, Tamil Nadu, India

All Rights Reserved

First Edition, 2025

Copyright © 2025, Muniswamy Rajakumar

All rights reserved. No part of this publication may be reproduced, distributed, or transmitted in any form or by any means, including photocopying, recording, or other electronic or mechanical methods, without the author's prior written permission. It is illegal to copy this book, post it to a website, or distribute it by any other means without permission.

The request for permission should be addressed to the author.

ISBN: 978-93-343-3079-3
Email:shreeshambav@gmail.com
Web:www.shambav.org

DEDICATION

"Isavasyam idam sarvam yat kim ca jagatyam jagat, tena tyaktena bhunjitha, ma gridhah kasyasvid dhanam"

To the Almighty,

the Divine Masters,

the family who listens,

and my parents who see –

your presence shapes the pages of my life's journey.

"Isavasyam idam sarvam yat kim ca jagatyam jagat"

Meaning: "God encompasses everything you perceive, see, or touch with your sense organs."

DISCLAIMER

The Law of Attraction: A Soulful Path presents a comprehensive and thoughtful examination of the fundamental principles underlying the Law of Attraction. Through twelve guiding rules, this work aims to empower readers to manifest their desires with clarity, emotional alignment, and purposeful action. The book offers insights drawn from both philosophical perspectives and practical applications to support personal transformation and fulfilment.

Readers are advised that the information contained herein is intended solely for educational and inspirational purposes. While every effort has been made to ensure the accuracy and integrity of the material, the author and publisher make no guarantees regarding specific outcomes or results. Manifestation and personal growth are deeply individual processes influenced by numerous factors beyond the scope of this book.

This work does not replace professional advice in medical, psychological, legal, or financial matters. Readers should consult qualified professionals before making any decisions or changes that could impact their wellbeing or circumstances.

By reading this book, the reader acknowledges personal responsibility for their application of its content and the ensuing consequences.

Note - If any part of the book, in any sequence, hurts the reader's sentiments, it would be just out of a sheer accident not intentional

EPIGRAM

"You are not waiting on the world to grant you life—
You are the quiet artist of reality.
What you believe, you invite.
What you feel, you form.
And what you love, becomes the world you live in."

— Shree Shambav

The Law of Attraction

A Soulful Path

Shree Shambav

Shree Shambav is a 45X best-selling author renowned
for his transformative works in personal development
and spiritual growth.

Dear Cherished Readers

Dear Cherished Readers,

As I embark on this new literary voyage, my heart swells with profound gratitude and an overwhelming sense of connection. With deep emotion, I extend my heartfelt appreciation to each of you who has joined me on this journey.

With sincere warmth, I invite you to revisit the steps we have taken together through the pages of my earlier works. Our odyssey began with "Journey of Soul - Karma," a book that marked my first foray into the world of words and a testament to the raw passion that ignited my writing adventure.

The subsequent chapters of our shared journey unfolded through the enchanting tapestry of the *"Twenty + One"* series. With each page turned, it felt as though a brushstroke was added to the canvas of our collective imagination—stories and sentiments woven to echo within the quiet corners of your heart. These weren't just words; they were invitations to feel, to reflect, and to remember what truly matters.

And how can I not cherish the transformative path we walked together through the *"Life Changing Journey— Inspirational Quotes Series?"* Day by day, quote by quote, we ventured inward—into spaces often overlooked— to find wisdom in simplicity and light in life's shadows. Each reflection was offered as a gentle whisper of hope, a spark meant to uplift, inspire, and remind us that even in silence, the soul speaks.

The release of "Death - Light of Life and the Shadow of Death" promises to shed new light on the timeless mystery of death.

The **Optimum Python Series** is a comprehensive guide designed to empower readers at every stage of their programming journey. It begins with *Series I: Ultimate Guide for Beginners*, which lays a strong foundation in Python, making it accessible and engaging for newcomers. *Series II: Exploring Data Structures and Algorithms* takes the next step, offering a deep dive into core computer science principles that enhance problem-solving skills and coding efficiency. Building on this, *Series III: Python Power for Data Science* introduces powerful libraries such as NumPy, Pandas, Matplotlib, and Scikit-learn, guiding readers through data manipulation, visualisation, and foundational machine learning techniques. Finally, *Series IV: Unleashing the Potential of Data Science with Machine Learning Techniques* explores advanced machine learning models and real-world applications, enabling readers to harness the full potential of data-driven insights. Whether you're just starting out or looking to master sophisticated tools and strategies, this series is your roadmap to Python proficiency and beyond.

Shree Shambav expands his artistic repertoire with *"Whispers of Eternity: A Symphony of Soulful Verses,"* a heartfelt exploration of the human experience. Alongside this, his *"Whispers of the Soul: A Journey Through Haiku"* distils profound insights into poignant verses. Together, these works showcase his versatility and mastery of soulful expression, inviting readers on a journey of self-discovery. Through his poetry, he weaves a rich tapestry of emotion that resonates deeply with the heart.

Shree Shambav's latest works—*Learn to Love Yourself: A Journey of Discovering Inner Beauty and Strength Through 10 Transformative Rules, The Power of Letting Go: Embrace Freedom and Happiness, A Journey of Lasting Peace*—are true treasures of self-discovery, *The Entitlement Trap: Get Over It, Get On, Whispers of a Dying Soul: Unspoken Regrets and Unlived Dreams, Whispers of Silence - Unlocking Inner Power through Stillness, The Power of Words: Transforming Speech, Transforming Lives, The Art of Intentional Living: Minimalism for a Life of Purpose, Awakening the Infinite:The Power of Consciousness in Transforming Life, Beyond the Veil: A Journey Through Life After Death series, Bonds Beyond Blood - Where love builds bridges, and bonds defy blood., A Journey into Spiritual Maturity - 12 Golden Rules for Inner*

Transformation, The Seeker's Gold : Unlocking Life's Greatest Treasure, , The Power of Manifestation - Unlocking The Path From Thought To Reality and Born to Rise Series.

In addition to these works, Shree Shambav has recently ventured into astrology with the release of Astrology Unveiled – Foundations of Ancient Wisdom Series I to VI, expanding into the realm of metaphysics. These books explore the foundational principles of Vedic astrology, offering readers a rich and practical understanding of this ancient wisdom.

Your unwavering support, enthusiasm to immerse yourself in my writings, and readiness to embark on these journeys with me have been my greatest sources of inspiration. Your input has been a beacon guiding me through the creation process, moulding these stories into containers of passion, emotion, knowledge, and resonance.

As I unveil this new narrative before you, know that your presence, insights, and shared moments have been my companions. The path we have walked together is etched in the annals of my creative evolution, and it's an honour beyond words to have you by my side once more.

Here's to the readers who have illuminated my path with their presence, who have embraced my stories with open hearts, and who have woven themselves into the very fabric of my literary world. Our journey has been a symbiotic dance of writer and reader, a harmony of souls brought together by the magic of storytelling.

With a heart brimming with appreciation and eyes glistening with anticipation, I extend my deepest gratitude for your unwavering support. Thank you for the memories, the shared emotions, and the countless hours spent in the worlds we've crafted together. As we step into this new adventure, let's continue to explore, feel, and discover the boundless horizons that words can unveil.

Warmly,

Shree Shambav

SHREE SHAMBAV

Suggested Reads

FROM BEST-SELLING AUTHOR

Endorsements

This book did not just inform me—it transformed me. In a world obsessed with quick fixes and surface-level affirmations, *The Law of Attraction: A Soulful Path* is a sacred invitation to return to what truly creates change: alignment of the heart, clarity of intent, and the courage to feel deeply. Shree Shambav's words don't shout—they whisper gently into the places you've forgotten to listen. This is not just a guide to manifestation; it is a journey back to yourself. With every chapter, I felt seen, softened, and strengthened. If you've ever longed for a more honest and emotionally grounded path to creating the life you desire, this book is your mirror, your map, and your medicine.

— Rohith, Advocate

About the Author

Shree Shambav is an internationally acclaimed bestselling author, inspirational speaker, artist, philanthropist, life coach, strategist and entrepreneur. A world record holder, his deep passion for music led him to create soul-stirring albums, drawing inspiration from his celebrated poetry collection, Whispers of Eternity. His profound insights have sparked deep personal transformations, guiding countless individuals toward self-discovery, purposeful living, and authenticity.

With an extraordinary ability to unlock human potential, Shree empowers individuals to break through limitations and embrace their highest selves. His writings, lectures, and compassionate guidance continue to uplift lives, fostering resilience, mindfulness, and personal growth.

Shree Shambav is a 45x best-selling author celebrated for his profound contributions to personal development and spiritual growth.

Shree Shambav's literary journey took flight with the celebrated Journey of Soul - Karma, where he delved into the depths of human experience to unveil profound insights. Garnering recognition through multiple literature awards, his repertoire includes esteemed works, such as the Twenty + One Series, and the enlightening Life Changing Journey – Inspirational Quotes series.

As a distinguished alumnus of the Indian Institute of Management and the National Institute of Technology, Shree Shambav brings a wealth of corporate acumen from his tenure in multinational corporations. His most recent publications, including Unveiling the Enigma, Death - Light of Life and the Shadow of Death and Optimum – Power Python Series I, Series II, Series III and Series IV, demonstrate his mastery of both the literary and technical spheres.

Shree Shambav expands his artistic repertoire with "*Whispers of Eternity: - A Symphony of Soulful Verses,*" a heartfelt exploration of the human experience. Alongside this, his "*Whispers of the Soul: A Journey Through Haiku*" distils profound insights into poignant verses. Together, these works showcase his versatility and mastery of soulful expression, inviting readers on a journey of self-discovery. Through his poetry, he weaves a rich tapestry of emotion that resonates deeply with the heart.

Shree Shambav's latest works—*Learn to Love Yourself: A Journey of Discovering Inner Beauty and Strength Through 10 Transformative Rules, The Power of Letting Go: Embrace Freedom and Happiness, A Journey of Lasting Peace—are true treasures of self-discovery, The Entitlement Trap: Get Over It, Get On, Whispers of a Dying Soul: Unspoken Regrets and Unlived Dreams, Whispers of Silence - Unlocking Inner Power through Stillness, The Power of Words: Transforming Speech, Transforming Lives, The Art of Intentional Living: Minimalism for a Life of Purpose, Awakening the Infinite: The Power of Consciousness in Transforming Life, Beyond the Veil: A Journey Through Life After Death series, Bonds Beyond Blood - Where love builds bridges, and bonds defy blood., A Journey into Spiritual Maturity - 12 Golden Rules for Inner Transformation, The Seeker's Gold : Unlocking Life's Greatest Treasure, The Power of Manifestation - Unlocking The Path From Thought To Reality and Born to Rise Series.*

In addition to these works, Shree Shambav has recently ventured into astrology with the release of Astrology Unveiled – Foundations of Ancient Wisdom Series I to VI, expanding into the realm of metaphysics. These books explore the foundational principles of Vedic astrology, offering readers a rich and practical understanding of this ancient wisdom.

Shree Shambav established the Ayur Rakshita Foundation, which is dedicated to promoting boundless growth, universal fraternity, and environmental protection. The charity helps diverse communities while working for societal progress.

To learn more about Shree Shambav and his works, visit his website at www.shambav.org. For information about the Ayur Rakshita Foundation and its initiatives, visit www.shambav-ayurrakshita.org.

Let's Follow him on Social Media: **@shreeshambav**

Main: https://linktr.ee/shreeshambav

Website: https://www.shambav.org/

LinkedIn: https://www.linkedin.com/in/shreeshambav/

Blog: https://blog.shambav.org/

Instagram: https://www.instagram.com/shreeshambav/

YouTube: https://www.youtube.com/@shreeshambav

Amazon: https://www.amazon.com/author/shreeshambav

Goodreads: https://www.goodreads.com/author/show/22367436.Shree_Shambav

PREFACE

A Journey from Within

There are moments in life when we sense something deeper stirring beneath the noise of our thoughts. Like a quiet ripple across still waters, it whispers not in words, but in feeling—in longing. It arrives when the world outside no longer matches the world we ache to live within.

This book was born in one of those moments.

We live in an age flooded with information, yet parched for inner wisdom. We scroll, we strive, we seek—but often, in the quiet chambers of our being, we wonder: *Is this all there is? Am I merely reacting to life, or can I become a conscious participant in its unfolding?* The Law of Attraction offers not just an answer—but a path.

Not a shortcut.

Not a fantasy.

A path.

One that leads inward, before it moves outward. A journey that asks us to become the vibration of what we desire—not by pretending or forcing—but by remembering who we truly are underneath the layers of fear, doubt, and limitation.

The Law of Attraction is often misunderstood as a tool to "get" what we want. But in truth, it is an invitation to *become* what we seek—to live in emotional alignment with our highest visions, and to act in trust from that sacred space. It is less about controlling life and more about co-creating with it.

Think of a seed in the soil. The seed cannot force the sun to shine, nor command the rain to fall. Yet it trusts—deeply—that life will meet it halfway, *if it dares to grow.* The same is true for us. Our dreams are seeds. Our thoughts, sunlight. Our emotions, water. Our actions, roots reaching down. When all parts align, the invisible becomes visible. And what once seemed impossible begins to take form.

This book is your garden journal.

Each chapter offers one rule—one sacred principle—to help you clear the soil of your mind, nourish the heart of your desire, and cultivate the spiritual muscle required for manifestation. You will not find empty promises here. Instead, you'll find grounded wisdom, emotional depth, soulful practices, and real-life reflections—because transformation is not a performance. It is a presence.

You'll learn how clarity sharpens intention, how emotion magnetises experience, and how inspired action makes the unseen seen. You'll walk with patience, dance with change, and return again and again to the most important truth: *You are not separate from the life you long for—you are its source.*

This book is not just meant to be read. It is meant to be lived. Breathed. Felt. Returned to, as a mirror and a map.

So begin this journey with courage and openness. Bring your past, your pain, your passion. Bring your desire—not just to attract things—but to awaken the creator within. As you turn these pages, may you turn inward. And as you turn inward, may your outer world begin to reflect the brilliance you were always meant to live.

Welcome to *The Soulful Path*.

Let's walk it together.

Shree Shambav

SHREE SHAMBAV

INTRODUCTION

Introduction: The Raindrop and the River

Imagine a single raindrop.

It falls quietly from the sky, unnoticed by most, vanishing into the soil or slipping into a crack on the earth. It's humble. Unremarkable. Yet that single drop, in union with countless others, carves canyons, nourishes roots, and eventually becomes the mighty river that feeds civilisations. Not by force, but by consistency. Not by noise, but by essence.

You are that raindrop.

Your thoughts, your emotions, your beliefs—each is a drop of water falling into the stream of your life.

What you think, you feel. What you feel, you radiate. And what you radiate... the world reflects back.

The Law of Attraction is not about wishing harder or trying to "think positive" while drowning inside. It is not magic, nor a shortcut to avoid pain or bypass life's complexity. It is something more tender, more powerful. It is **a remembering**—that your inner world creates your outer one, and that your soul holds the blueprint for a life rich with purpose, connection, and joy.

Why This Book?

So many teachings on the Law of Attraction speak only to the mind: change your thoughts, envision success, speak affirmations. But when the heart aches, when life feels heavy and your dreams distant, the mind alone cannot carry you forward. You need a soul. You need presence. You need a path that honours both your **yearning** and your **becoming**.

This book is that path.

The Law of Attraction: A Soulful Path is divided into three parts:

- **Part I: Foundations of Attraction** helps you awaken the inner forces that shape your reality—your thoughts, emotions, energy, and beliefs.

- **Part II: The Journey Within** invites you to release resistance, confront subconscious blocks, and reclaim your power through patience, action, and self-trust.

- **Part III: Living the Attraction** guides you to radiate your alignment outward—through gratitude, love, influence, and change.

Each rule is not just a mental concept, but a soul invitation—paired with practical exercises, reflections, and rituals to ground the invisible into the tangible.

A Soulful Journey

To follow this path is to stop waging war on yourself.

It is to replace "fixing" with **honouring**, "trying" with **trusting**, and "waiting" with **welcoming**.

It is to become not just a goal-setter, but a co-creator with life itself.

You may find, as you move through these pages, that the desires you once chased start to flow toward you, not because you did more, but because you **became more**. Aligned. Open. Ready.

Let this book be a gentle hand on your shoulder and a mirror to your deeper truth.

Let it remind you:

You are not here to force your way through life.

You are here to align, to feel, to act, to receive.

You are here to live a magnetic life—one where love is the current and your soul, the compass.

So, begin not with striving, but with presence.

Let the raindrop fall.

Let it ripple.

Let it rise.

Let us begin—

The Soul's Magnet

A whisper stirs where silence grows,
Where dreams begin but no one knows.
Beyond the veil of thought and fear,
A deeper voice is drawing near.
Not loud, not fast, but soft and true—
It speaks: *"The world reflects back to you."*

Each thought, a seed beneath your skin,
Each feeling, the wind that shapes within.
What you believe becomes your sky,
What you resist will still reply.
The soul does not forget your name—
It waits until you light the flame.

Intent is more than wish or goal—
It's what you feed your waking soul.
A single breath of truth, held tight,

Can move the stars, can birth new light.
When visions bloom in heart and hand,
The unseen answers your command.

But not by force, and not by fear—
The way is paved when you are clear.
The joy you give, the love you share,
Becomes the bridge from thought to prayer.
It's not the shout that shifts the air,
But quiet trust, held firm with care.

Let not delay undo your grace—
Each moment finds its perfect place.
The seed does not bloom overnight,
But turns to sun, then breaks to light.
So water hope with gentle breath—
The law is life, not fate or death.

You are the mirror and the flame,
The calling voice, the guiding name.
Not just a dreamer chasing skies—
But soul in form, both wise and wise.

So think with love, and walk in peace—
The life you long for will increase.

— **Shree Shambav**

PROLOGUE

The Invisible Thread

There is a moment—quiet, unassuming—when something within you stirs.

It's not thunderous. It doesn't announce itself with lightning or loud applause.

It arrives like the first breath of dawn—soft, subtle, yet undeniably present.

That moment is a call.

Not from the world outside, but from within.

From a place in your soul that remembers something the mind has forgotten:

You were never meant to live by accident. You were born to live *on purpose*.

Most of us wander through life like ships without anchors, pulled by the tides of circumstance, tossed by winds of doubt and desire. We chase dreams that aren't ours, carry burdens that were never meant to be held, and wonder why we feel lost even in a room full of direction.

But beneath it all, like a current beneath the surface, there flows an invisible thread—a magnetic pull between who we are and who we are becoming.

The Law of Attraction is not about wishful thinking or magical solutions.

It is the name we give to that sacred dance between intention and reality.

Between inner vibration and outer experience.

Think of your life as a garden.

Your thoughts are seeds. Your emotions, the sun and rain.

Your actions till the soil.

And your beliefs? They are the climate in which everything grows—or withers.

You cannot grow roses in frozen soil.

You cannot plant doubt and expect to harvest peace.

And yet, you can turn barren ground into a blooming field with enough love, light, and time.

This book is not just about how to manifest a new job, partner, or opportunity—though all of that is possible.

It's about becoming someone who no longer chases light, because you *remember* you are the light.

It's about aligning the soul, the mind, and the heart— so that the universe mirrors back your truth instead of your fears.

Each rule in this book is a stepping stone across a river of transformation.

Some will challenge your patterns.

Some will soothe your wounds.

All will ask you to return to your centre.

Because manifestation is not just an act of asking.

It is an act of becoming.

So wherever you are right now—whatever doubts you carry, whatever dreams still whisper—know this:

You are not starting over.

You are simply coming home.

And the path begins here.

With you.

With belief.

With the willingness to become who you were always meant to be.

— *Shree Shambav*

CONTENTS

DEDICATION	iii
DISCLAIMER	v
EPIGRAM	vii
Dear Cherished Readers	xi
Suggested Reads	xvi
Endorsements	xvii
About the Author	xix
PREFACE	xxv
INTRODUCTION	xxix
The Soul's Magnet	xxxiii
PROLOGUE	xxxvii
CONTENTS	xli
At Kumbhariyur	45
The Dance Between Stillness and Creation	45
PART ONE	61
Foundations of Attraction	61
CHAPTER I	63
Understanding the Law of Attraction	63
CHAPTER II	79

Rule 1 – Clarity of Intent 79
CHAPTER III 95
Rule 2 – Positive Thinking 95
CHAPTER IV 113
Rule 3 – Emotional Alignment 113
PART TWO 131
The Journey Within 131
Releasing, Realigning, and Reclaiming 131
CHAPTER V 133
Rule 4 – Taking Inspired Action 133
CHAPTER VI 149
Rule 5 – Letting Go of Resistance 149
CHAPTER VII 163
Rule 6 – The Power of Belief 163
CHAPTER VIII 183
Rule 7 – Cultivating Patience and Persistence 183
PART THREE 203
Living the Attraction 203
Integration, Radiance, and Legacy 203
CHAPTER IX 205
Rule 8 – Practising Gratitude 205
CHAPTER X 219

Rule 9 – Surrounding Yourself with Positive Influences 219

CHAPTER XI 239

Rule 10 – Embracing Change 239

CHAPTER XII 255

Rule 11 – Consistent Practice and Dedication 255

CHAPTER XIII 271

Rule 12 – Spreading Love and Positivity 271

Final Chapter 285

The Magnetic Life 285

Epilogue 301

APPENDICES 305

APPENDICES A 307

Living the Magnetic Life 307

Life Coach and Philanthropist 313

TESTIMONIALS 317

ACKNOWLEDGEMENTS 327

At Kumbhariyur

The Dance Between Stillness and Creation

"The universe listens to your vibration, but it moves for your devotion."

- Shree Shambav

The morning in Kumbhariyur felt less like time passing and more like time pausing to pray.

As the dew-laced grass kissed their bare feet and mist curled like incense around their ankles, the group moved through the silence like pilgrims within a living temple. Every leaf seemed dipped in blessing. Every breath felt sacred.

When **Akshaya's voice** gently broke the reverence—*"Guruji will be taking a session on Law of Attraction…"*—it didn't disrupt the moment. It deepened it. It was as though even the fog paused to listen.

Apeksha's eyes flickered, not in surprise, but in remembrance. Her hand instinctively rested against her heart.

Nita noticed. "Apeksha, why not narrate an incident from your previous retreat?"

She nodded slowly, her voice tender. "Yes... and so did I."

Apeksha's Story: The Potter and the Mirror

Apeksha's voice was soft but steady, like a stream remembering the path it once carved into stone.

"It was my second retreat with Guruji," she began. "We were in the hills of Rishikesh. On the third morning, Guruji told us a story. He said—'There was once a potter who made a mirror. But instead of placing it before the sun to reflect light, he kept it buried in a box, hidden from dust. Every day he prayed, hoping it would shine. He believed in the mirror, but he never gave it a chance to meet the light.'"

She paused, looking at the rising sun now painting the mist gold.

"That day," she continued, "I realised I was the potter. I believed in dreams, in purpose, in possibilities—but I kept them buried beneath fear, doubt, and hesitation. The **Law of Attraction** was not just about thinking good thoughts. It was about *letting the mirror out*, placing it in the light of action, clarity, and emotional truth."

Vasudeva leaned in, visibly moved. "And what changed for you after that?"

Apeksha smiled. "I stopped asking, *When will my life change?* and started asking, *'Am I allowing life to reach me?'*"

She turned to them with gentleness. "The law doesn't just respond to your desires. It responds to your readiness. To your alignment."

The Path to Buddha Hall

By now, their feet had taken them along the stone path toward the Buddha Hall, but the story had taken them inward.

Akanksh, who had quietly seated himself beneath the old banyan, added, "Maybe we don't manifest by chasing... maybe we manifest by becoming."

Kiran glanced at his watch, then back at the shimmering canopy. "Time for the session," he said, but even that reminder felt like a sacred line in a poem.

Their walk toward the Buddha Hall was not hurried. It was ceremonial.

With each footstep, it felt less like moving through space and more like moving through presence.

Inside the Buddha Hall

The hall was a vessel of silence, holding the breaths and expectations of every devotee present. The floor was cool beneath the mats. Incense curled in gentle spirals. Morning light streamed through the high windows, casting soft halos across the space.

After a few quiet minutes, Guruji entered.

His robe swayed like a breeze in human form. He moved with the serenity of someone who had forgotten the noise of time. He bowed to the space, then sat on his asana. Eyes closed. Breath merged with stillness.

And when his eyes finally opened, they carried the whole sky inside them.

His smile wasn't just warm—it was illuminating, as if the universe had chosen this very moment to speak through him.

"We begin," he said, "not by asking what we want to attract… but by who we are becoming in the process."

Apeksha asked, "Guruji, what is the difference between the Power of Manifestation and the Law of Attraction?" She asked, gently breaking the silence that had become prayer.

The Seed and the Garden

Guruji, after a pause, said, "Apeksha," he said softly, "imagine you are holding a seed in your hand. It is a seed of fragrant jasmine. In that tiny speck of life lies the promise of a blooming garden. But a promise alone does not birth petals."

"The **Law of Attraction** is like the soil, the sun, the rain—it responds to your energy. If your thoughts, emotions, and beliefs are in harmony with love, peace, or abundance, then that becomes the climate in which your desires can grow. It is **the response of the universe to your frequency.**"

"But the **Power of Manifestation** is the choice to **plant that seed.** To not merely wish for a garden, but to step into the sacred act of creation. You plant, water, tend to it—you co-create with the divine."

The Mirror and the Sculptor

Guruji's voice was gentle, but his words carved through the fog of illusion like morning sunlight through mist.

"The Law of Attraction is like a mirror—it reflects who you are being. If you live in the vibration of fear, you attract more fear. If you radiate love, it echoes back to you. It's passive—it responds to what you already carry within."

"But Manifestation," Guruji said, watching the ripples, "is the ripple-maker. You don't wait for reflection—you create movement. You sculpt your inner world to match your outer longing. You act with intention, speak with clarity, and walk with faith even before the path reveals itself. It's not passive attraction. It's active becoming."

The Boat and the Wind

He picked up a dry leaf.

"Let me tell you a story," Guruji said. "There once was a young seeker standing by a river. Her dreams—peace, truth, love—waited across the water. She prayed for the wind to come and carry her across. The universe heard. The wind came. But her boat remained still."

"Why?" he asked, looking into Apeksha's eyes. "Because she hadn't untied the rope. She hadn't placed her hands on the oar. She hadn't believed that her own movement was part of the miracle."

"The Law of Attraction is the wind—it will come when you are aligned.

The Power of Manifestation is untying the rope, lifting the sail, and saying yes to the journey."

The Sacred Dance of Faith and Action

Guruji's voice was now almost a whisper—meant not for the ears, but for the soul.

"You see, manifestation is not about waiting for magic. It is about becoming magical. It's not about hoping something comes. It's about becoming someone who deserves, welcomes, and holds what is meant to come."

He touched his chest with his palm.

"The Law of Attraction rearranges the universe to meet your vibration.

The Power of Manifestation rearranges you to meet your destiny."

He closed his eyes briefly, then opened them with a radiant calm.

"Together, they form a sacred dance—stillness and movement, faith and form, trust and transformation."

Guruji looked at Apeksha with the tenderness of one who sees not just the seeker—but the seed of transformation within them.

"Apeksha," he began again, his voice carrying the warmth of a morning sun dissolving the last trace of night's chill, "you spoke of dreams—of business, love, and the soul's journey. Let me now guide you through the path between dreaming and becoming."

He turned slightly, gesturing with his hand, as if painting on the canvas of still air.

"Imagine the **Law of Attraction** as the **sunlight**—always shining, always present. It nourishes whatever it touches, whether weeds or wildflowers. It does not choose—it responds. You bring your energy, your thoughts, your feelings, and it magnifies them."

"But the **Power of Manifestation**," he paused, gently tapping his heart, "is the gardener in you. It is the sacred choice to prepare the soil, to plant the seed, to water it with daily devotion, and to remove the weeds of doubt and fear. **You are not merely attracting—you are co-creating.**"

The Boat and the Builder

"Let me tell you a story," Guruji said, his eyes twinkling.

"There once was a young woman named Shobha who lived by a vast ocean. On the far shore were her dreams—freedom, meaning, a life she had longed for. Every morning, she stood at the shore, offering prayers for a boat, hoping the ocean would carry her across."

"And one day, the tide brought her driftwood. Then rope. Then the tools. She rejoiced. The universe had heard her."

"But days passed, and the boat never came fully built. She grew disheartened."

"Then an old mystic passed by and said, 'Shobha, the universe has given you what you need—not what you want. **Now you must build the boat.**'"

Guruji smiled.

"That, Apeksha, is the Power of Manifestation. The Law of Attraction gives you the raw material. The Power of Manifestation is your willingness to shape it with vision, belief, and consistent action."

Real-Life Applications

Guruji spoke in a rhythm, like a sacred chant made practical:

1. Career Growth

Law of Attraction:

"You align with abundance. You focus on thriving. You hold gratitude in your heart. This opens doors—an unexpected email, a mentor crossing your path."

Power of Manifestation:

"You choose a clear destination. You say—'I will become Creative Director in 12 months.' You visualise it daily. You build your skills, update your portfolio, and apply fearlessly. You become the person that the future demands."

Daily Devotionals:

- Morning Visualisation: Feel yourself succeeding.
- Action Step: One tangible move daily—learning, networking, creating.
- Night Gratitude: 3 wins, no matter how small.

Affirmation:
"Success flows through my clarity, courage, and commitment."

2. Love & Relationships

Law of Attraction:

"You radiate love. You forgive your past. You become emotionally available to receive."

Power of Manifestation:

"You script your desires with precision. Not a checklist—but a feeling. You affirm it. You heal your heart. You show up open. You become the love you seek."

Daily Devotionals:

- Mirror Work: "I love and accept you."
- Journaling: Write the essence of the partner and the life you are co-creating.
- Release Ritual: Breathe out yesterday's pain.

Affirmation:

"I am worthy of love that is whole, healing, and divine."

3. Spiritual Growth

Law of Attraction:

"You focus on divine connection. You attune to peace. Life sends you signs—books, guides, synchronicities."

Power of Manifestation:

"You set a soul-intention. You meditate. You study. You surrender to the rhythm of the divine. You become an instrument of the sacred."

Daily Devotionals:

- Morning Stillness: Sit with breath.
- Nourishment: Read, reflect, listen to sacred truths.
- Journal Synchronicities: Dreams, patterns, messages from life.

Affirmation:
"I am unfolding into the sacred truth of who I am."

Guruji looked around the Buddha Hall. A soft breeze moved through the open windows like a blessing.

"You see," he said, "**The Law of Attraction is the invitation. The Power of Manifestation is your RSVP to destiny.** One opens the door. The other walks you through it."

He placed his hand over his heart.

"And remember, Apeksha—**the universe rearranges the world around you. But manifestation rearranges the world within you.** That's where miracles are born."

A deep silence filled the space, not empty—but alive. A sacred hush where truth had spoken.

Apeksha bowed her head—not in confusion, but in clarity. Not in longing, but in reverence.

Outside, a jasmine petal fell gently onto the earth.

As if the universe had just whispered, "Yes."

Concept	Law of Attraction	Power of Manifestation
Nature	Universal principle	Conscious process
Focus	Attraction through thoughts and emotions	Creation through intent and aligned action
Activity	More receptive	More proactive
Tools	Mindset, emotional vibration	Visualisation, scripting, action, belief

A Tear, A Truth, and a Jasmine-Scented

Apeksha sat still. Her breath was no longer just breath—it was a rhythm in tune with something larger, something eternal. A single tear traced the curve of her cheek, not from sorrow, but from truth remembered.

She was no longer hoping for change.

She had become the change.

She no longer wished for the garden.

She had become the gardener.

The Weaver Within

The incense curled upward like silent prayers, carrying with it the scent of sandalwood and jasmine. The golden morning light filtered gently through the tall windows of **Buddha Hall**, brushing the marble floor in long, reverent strokes. Silence hung in the air, not as an absence of sound, but as a living presence.

Padma's voice broke the silence with a question that felt less like inquiry and more like longing.

"Guruji, what are the dominant thought patterns we entertain daily, and how might they be shaping the results we see in our lives?"

Guruji closed his eyes for a moment, and when he opened them, there was a soft glint—not just of wisdom, but of memory.

"Padma," he said, "let me share a story that was first told to me in silence, and only then in words."

"In a small village much like our Kumbhariyur," Guruji began, his voice echoing gently off the stone walls of the Buddha Hall, "there lived an old woman known simply as Amma. She wasn't a healer, or a priestess, or a teacher. She was a weaver. But not of cloth—of meaning."

"Every morning, before the birds stirred and the river yawned open to the sky, she would sit by her loom. And with each thread she chose—she was not just making a shawl, but weaving her story. A golden thread for joy. Indigo for sorrow. Crimson for love. Ivory for silence."

"She believed that the cloth she wove would one day wrap her soul on its final journey—not because it was beautiful, but because it told the truth of who she had become."

Guruji looked around the hall. "But here is what moved me most—it was the threads she used most often that dominated the weave. Not the rare moments, but the daily thoughts."

The Mirror of Thought

"Our daily thought patterns," Guruji continued, "are like those threads. You may speak of peace once a week, but if you think in anxiety every morning, guess which colour your soul's shawl will wear?"

"Your outer life, Padma, is nothing more than the inner fabric made visible."

He leaned slightly forward, his tone tender.

"If your dominant thoughts are resentment, fear, or unworthiness—they do not just visit. They plant themselves. They build homes. And then… they decorate your reality."

Analogy: The Lighthouse in the Fog

"Let me offer you another picture," Guruji said, his fingers drawing an imaginary beam in the air.

"Imagine Buddha Hall surrounded in fog. Dense, thick, disorienting. Now imagine a lighthouse standing just outside, its beam cutting through the mist. That beam is like your dominant thought. It cannot remove the fog—but it helps you see your way through it."

"Most people live in fog. But those who become aware of their thinking—they become the lighthouse."

The Inner Ritual

Guruji's voice softened to a whisper, as if speaking directly to Padma's heart.

"Every morning, I ask myself: What is the fragrance I wish to carry today? Is it gratitude or judgment? Stillness, or control? I align not just my schedule, but my soul."

He looked up, and silence returned—not heavy, but healing.

"Your dominant thought is not just a habit—it is a magnet. It pulls life toward you. It shapes your emotions, your relationships, your prayers, and even your delays."

Guruji smiled, "To know your dominant thought is to meet the hidden author of your days. To change it—not forcefully, but lovingly—is to choose a new future, moment by moment."

And as a breeze moved gently through the open arches of the Buddha Hall, it carried with it not just coolness—but a clarity that touched every heart in the room.

PART ONE

Foundations of Attraction

Awakening the Inner World

"True transformation begins not in changing the outside, but in awakening the vast, silent universe within—where the soul's wisdom quietly shapes the reality beyond."

-Shree Shambav

CHAPTER I

Understanding the Law of Attraction

"Every thought is a silent wave cast into the ocean of reality— rippling outward to meet you again as life."

– Shree Shambav

Synopsis

Every transformation begins with awareness. This chapter lays the foundational understanding of the Law of Attraction by unveiling the invisible threads that connect thought, emotion, and energy. We explore how your inner world shapes your outer experiences—how your thoughts become vibrations, how those vibrations influence outcomes, and how your beliefs silently govern what you allow yourself to receive.

Rooted in both spiritual wisdom and emerging science, this chapter invites you to step into the role of a conscious co-creator. It offers insights into the power of mindset, the emotional energy you emit, and how reality often mirrors the story you tell yourself. Whether you're a sceptic or a seeker, this chapter opens the door to seeing life not as a series of random events, but as a reflection of your own energetic blueprint.

Akshaya, seated with hands folded, his gaze calm but curious, gently raised his voice: "Guruji, how does our current emotional state influence our decisions, relationships, and opportunities?"

A hush followed—*not of silence, but of depth.*

Guruji turned slightly to him, his eyes tender with recognition. He didn't answer right away. He simply *breathed*, as if calling upon the wisdom of the earth beneath them.

The River Beneath the Skin

"Akshaya," Guruji began, "emotions are not clouds that pass through you. They are rivers that shape your inner land."

"Most people believe that emotions are reactions, momentary. But I tell you—they are architects. They sculpt your perception. They paint your world. They decide whether you knock gently on a door… or walk away from it entirely."

He paused, letting the words linger like incense. "If your inner emotion is fear, every opportunity will seem like a threat. If it is joy, even uncertainty becomes adventure."

The Coloured Lens

Guruji reached for the simple spectacles resting on his knee. He lifted them gently.

"Imagine these lenses," he said. "If I tint them red, the world looks fiery. If I tint them blue, the world seems calm. The *world hasn't changed—only the lens has.*"

"Your emotions are those lenses. You do not see life as it is. You see life as *you are in that moment.*"

"Every decision—whether to stay or leave, to speak or remain silent, to risk or retreat—is coloured by the feeling you carry in that very breath."

The Sculptor and the Storm

"Let me share a story," Guruji continued, placing the spectacles back down.

"In an ancient kingdom, there was a sculptor who had mastered the art of shaping stone into soul. One day, as he was chiselling a divine form from marble, a sudden storm gathered. Thunder roared. Lightning cracked."

"His apprentice ran to him, terrified. 'Master, shall we seek shelter?'"

"But the sculptor kept carving, his hands steady, his breath calm. He smiled and said, 'The storm is loud, but it cannot touch my hands unless I let it inside.'"

Guruji looked around the Buddha Hall, then said softly:

"The sculptor's calm became his clarity. That sculpture—created amidst chaos—became the kingdom's treasure."

"But imagine, Akshaya, if he had allowed fear to enter? His hand would have trembled. The sculpture would have cracked. Not because of the storm—but because of the storm *within*."

The Magnetic Field of Emotion

"Your emotional state," Guruji said, "is a vibration. It is not static. It broadcasts. Like a magnetic field around your body—it *calls in* and *pushes away*."

"When you live in the emotion of gratitude, you attract more reasons to be grateful. When you carry anger unprocessed, you notice more triggers. Emotion is frequency. And *frequency is fate*."

Practical Insight: The Emotional Tuning Fork

Guruji raised his index finger thoughtfully.

"If you wish to attract joy, become joyful first. If you wish for love, let your heart be open first. If you seek clarity, become still within."

Guruji offered the analogy gently: "A tuning fork, when struck, makes another nearby fork vibrate at the same note. Emotion is your internal tuning fork. Life vibrates back."

The Inner Altar

The morning sun had now fully entered the Buddha Hall, lighting up the face of every seeker. Akshaya sat motionless, his chest rising and falling with a quiet reverence.

Guruji said: "So, before you make a decision, before you speak to a loved one, before you step into the world—pause. Ask yourself not what you are doing, but *what you are feeling*. Because that emotion is the real author of your action."

He looked at Akshaya and smiled—a smile that carried both grace and gravity.

"Decisions are not just made in the mind. They are first made in the heart's weather."

Vasudeva bowed gently and asked, "Guruji, in what ways have our beliefs—whether empowering or limiting—dictated what we believe is possible for us?"

Guruji smiled—not with quickness, but with the kind of grace that comes from understanding the weight of a question. He looked up for a moment, as though consulting something vast and ancient not outside him, but within.

He began in a voice that didn't break the silence, but extended it.

"Vasudeva… our beliefs are the soil in which the seeds of our destiny are sown. They do not merely shape what we think; they define what we dare to imagine. And that is the silent boundary of what we believe is possible."

He paused, then gently reached for a bowl of water before him. He placed a small stone inside and watched as it sank to the bottom.

"Imagine this water is your life," he said. "And the stone is a belief. Whether the belief says, 'I am not worthy of love' or 'Abundance is my birthright,' it will settle and colour everything above it. Every choice, every emotion, every risk we do or do not take—flows from that."

The Invisible Gatekeeper

Guruji leaned forward, eyes steady, voice soft. "There was once a young elephant, tied to a small wooden stake in the ground with a thin rope. As a calf, he tried countless times to pull free, but he could not. He grew up believing the stake was stronger than him. Years later, even when he had the strength to uproot trees, he never tried to break the rope. Why? Because the belief had already won the battle that strength could not."

He let the words settle, like petals on water. "You see, Vasudeva… the strongest prisons are not made of iron. They are woven from stories we once believed were true."

The Alchemy of Empowering Beliefs

"But just as limiting beliefs bind us, empowering ones liberate us," Guruji continued. "I once met a young woman who was told all her life that she was too sensitive, too emotional to survive in the real world. But one day, she turned that story around. She said, 'What if my sensitivity is my strength?' She became a healer, a poet, a light. Her belief gave birth to a new world—not outside her, but through her."

Guruji said with a smile, "Every belief is a brushstroke on the canvas of our becoming. You cannot paint a sunrise with a palette of doubt."

Guruji's voice softened further, almost like a whisper shared by the soul itself:

"We must ask ourselves—whose voice shaped this belief I carry? Was it a parent? A teacher? A moment of pain? And do I still choose to believe it now?"

He placed a hand over his heart and said, "When we challenge a limiting belief, we do not just shift our thoughts. We reclaim a lost part of ourselves—the part that always knew we were infinite."

There was stillness after his words. Not the absence of sound—but the presence of something sacred. Vasudeva lowered his head, not from shame, but from reverence. A tear welled up—not out of sadness, but from recognition.

In that moment, he wasn't just the listener of a truth—he became its witness.

Vidyarthi, always earnest and contemplative, asked, "Guruji, if thoughts carry energy and create reality, what mental diet are we feeding our future with?"

There was a still pause before the response came—not from delay, but reverence.

Guruji looked at him with a gaze that softened the soul and said gently, "Vidyarthi… imagine this—your thoughts are like seeds. Every word you tell yourself, every idea you entertain, every image you replay is a seed sown into the soil of your becoming. But more importantly—your thoughts are also your daily diet. And just as what you eat shapes your body, what you think nourishes or poisons your future."

The Garden and the Garbage

Guruji continued, his voice both gentle and piercing. "Let me tell you a story. There was once a man who wished to grow a beautiful garden filled with roses, jasmine, and tulsi. But every morning, instead of watering the soil with clean water, he poured into it dirty sewage—old thoughts, fears, judgments, resentments. He didn't realise that while the soil was fertile, it could not be discerned. It simply accepted what it was given and grew accordingly."

"In a few months, he found weeds, thorns, and decay. He wept and said, 'Why has my garden betrayed me?' But the garden only reflected his offerings. It bloomed what it was fed."

Guruji said softly, "This is our mind. The most fertile ground in all creation. It will grow whatever we consistently plant—be it faith or fear, truth or illusion."

The Silent Saboteur: Mindless Consumption

"Every complaint you rehearse, every news piece soaked in fear you consume without awareness, every comparison you indulge in on a glowing screen—these are not small things. They are meals served to your subconscious. And your future is being built with that fuel."

Vidyarthi sat still, his breath catching slightly as the realisation landed.

Guruji leaned forward and said, "If your thoughts today are shaping the weather of your life tomorrow—what kind of climate are you preparing? Storm or sunrise?"

The Potter's Apprentice

"There was a young potter's apprentice," Guruji said, "who was told he would never amount to anything. He believed it. He carried the voices of his critics in his head like sacred scriptures. Every time he shaped a pot, his hands trembled. The clay collapsed. One day, his master stopped him and said, 'Son, whose words are you kneading into the clay? Yours? Or the world's?'"

"The boy was stunned. He had never questioned the voices in his head. From that day on, he started to whisper affirmations as he worked: *I am steady. I am capable. I am enough.* Slowly, his hands grew sure. His art transformed. But more than the clay, it was he who was remoulded."

Conscious Mental Nutrition

Guruji, after a pause, said, "You brush your teeth every morning—but do you cleanse your mind? You nourish your body with food—but do you feed your future with faith?"

Guruji said, "Choose thoughts that build, not break. Thoughts that nourish, not numb. Thoughts that free, not fear."

Morning Interlude – Beneath the Banyan Tree

The morning discourse in Buddha Hall had stirred something profound in each heart. Now, as the session paused for a break, the sacred silence dissolved into gentle chatter and warm laughter.

Guruji rose quietly from his seat and said with a soft smile, "Let's pause for coffee. Let the mind absorb through the heart before we continue."

One by one, the devotees stepped out into the open. The air was cool and kissed with the faint fragrance of wild basil and the earth's dew. Birds chirped from the mango trees, and a light breeze stirred the leaves of the grand banyan tree nearby. It was not just a break—it was a return to the rhythm of being.

Akshaya and Apeksha brought trays of coffee and tea from the cottage. The steam rose like incense, curling into the cool air. Cups were passed around, and everyone settled beneath the sprawling banyan, its roots descending like blessings from the heavens.

Vidyarthi lay back on the grass, watching the sky through the branches. Padma leaned against a stone, sipping tea slowly. Vasudeva and Kiran were deep in quiet smiles and thoughts.

Apeksha, cradling her own cup, looked around. Something in the peace of the moment nudged a memory awake.

"Shall I share a story?" she asked, her voice soft but steady.

Everyone turned to her with anticipation.

The Fire in Kanchipuram

Apeksha held her cup gently, her fingers wrapped around its warmth like it held more than just coffee—like it held a memory waiting to be unwrapped.

"It was many years ago," she began, her voice quiet but steady, "in the temple town of Kanchipuram, during one of Guruji's early retreats. I still remember the scent of jasmine in the air, the chants echoing between the stone walls, the hush of devotion that blanketed us all."

She paused and looked up toward the swaying banyan leaves, as if something in their rhythm was helping her recall.

"That afternoon, the temple kitchen caught fire. At first, it was just a curl of smoke, faint and distant. But then the wind shifted, and flames danced into the open, wild and hungry. Panic rose like a second fire—louder, more contagious."

The listeners froze, the cups in their hands forgotten.

"People screamed. Some ran. Others froze. Even I, after years of meditation, felt my breath leave me. My hands trembled. It was as if the fire outside had awakened an older fire inside—fear. Ancient, irrational, and powerful."

Her eyes softened, shimmering with both vulnerability and reverence.

"And then—Guruji stood."

She said this simply, but something in her tone made the moment sacred.

"He didn't shout. He didn't rush. He didn't retreat. He *stood*. Like a mountain wrapped in silence. His eyes, calm. His posture, rooted. And something changed. Not just around him, but *within us*. It was as if the flames paused to listen."

Apeksha's voice became more melodic now, drawing everyone deeper into the story.

"He gently told the staff what to do. Directed the villagers without commanding them. He found the priest's son, who had been trapped behind a fallen cart, and carried him out—his robe brushing embers, yet untouched. In less than fifteen minutes, the fire was out."

There was reverence in the silence that followed. Even the breeze seemed to hush.

"That evening," Apeksha continued, "we sat beneath the old peepal tree, the sky still carrying the scent of charred wood and the memory of fear. I turned to Guruji and asked, 'Weren't you afraid?'"

Padma leaned forward, whispering, "And what did he say?"

Apeksha's lips curved into a smile of remembrance.

"He looked at me—not above me, but into me—and said, *When you become the stillness in the centre of the storm, even the storm remembers its silence.*"

The Lesson Beneath the Smoke

There was silence beneath the banyan once again, but this time, it wasn't the silence of speechlessness—it was the silence of being moved.

"That day," Apeksha continued gently, "I learned that wisdom is not just in speaking the right words or quoting scriptures. It's in presence. In how we *become* when the fire comes—whether literal or emotional. Guruji didn't just put out a fire—he showed us how to become the space that holds both fire and calm."

She gazed around at each devotee seated under the tree, now caught in a spell not of stories, but of remembrance.

"Life will always bring sparks—loss, uncertainty, rejection. But we are not here to run from them. We are here to respond—not from fear, but from stillness. Guruji didn't fight the fire. He *became* peace within it. And through that peace, it surrendered."

Her voice dropped to a whisper.

"Since that day, whenever a fire rises in my life, I ask myself—not how to escape it, but *how to remember my stillness in the middle of it.*"

The tea was cold now, but no one minded. Their hearts were warm.

Apeksha stood, brushing dew from her sari, and looked up at the sky beginning to brighten.

"And just like that," she said, "the fire that once threatened to consume us… became the very flame that illuminated the truth."

Akshaya looked at her and said quietly, "And Guruji… became the mirror through which we saw the calm we forgot we carried."

CHAPTER II

Rule 1 – Clarity of Intent

"When your intent is clear, the path appears—not because the world changes, but because you finally know where to look."

– Shree Shambav

Synopsis

Manifestation begins with direction. Without clarity, intention becomes scattered, like sunlight unfocused through glass. This chapter explores the transformative power of clearly defining what you truly desire—not just from your mind, but from the depth of your soul. When goals are aligned with emotional truth and soul purpose, they gain the magnetic force needed to draw life's opportunities closer.

You'll learn how to articulate your goals with precision through SMART goal-setting, how to engage your imagination through visualisation, and how to externalise your desires via vision boards. This isn't just about dreaming big—it's about becoming precise in your dreaming. When intention becomes clear, the universe doesn't just listen—it responds with precision.

The soft scent of sandalwood lingered in the still air of Buddha Hall. Light streamed through the high windows, casting golden patterns on the floor like blessings poured from heaven. Devotees in silence, hearts wide open, minds gently surrendered to the moment.

Apeksha's voice rose gently, a ripple in the sacred stillness. "Guruji," *she said, her gaze steady yet tender,* "are our current goals truly our own… or have they been shaped by others' expectations and the fear of being left behind?"

A hush followed. Even the wind outside seemed to pause, as if to listen.

Guruji looked at her not with answers—but with a knowing. The kind of knowing born not of books, but of silent mountains, long walks under stars, and the tear that never falls but always speaks.

He closed his eyes briefly, then opened them—reflecting not thought, but presence.

The Song and the Cage

"Apeksha," Guruji began, "let me tell you a story."

"There was once a nightingale, born in the heart of a deep forest. Its song was pure—so pure that even the river paused to listen. But one day, travellers came and heard the bird sing. They brought a golden cage, carved from riches and coated with admiration, and said, 'Come, sing for kings. The world must hear your beauty.' The nightingale, flattered and curious, stepped in."

"Days passed. The cage gleamed, and the bird sang... but something began to fade. The song, once free, now had undertones of longing. One day, the bird fell silent."

He looked at Apeksha with a gentleness that reached beyond the surface.

"Many of us," he said, "are like that nightingale. We step into the golden cage of approval, validation, trends, and timelines not truly ours. We chase degrees because the world praises them. We set goals not because our soul whispers them—but because society shouts them."

The Mirror of Intention

Guruji continued, "To know if a goal is truly yours, sit in silence and ask: *Would I still want this if no one else ever knew I achieved it?* If the answer is yes—then that is your soul's whisper. But if the joy fades in the absence of praise, applause, or Instagram likes, then you are walking someone else's path in your shoes."

He paused, letting the silence stretch like a sacred thread across the room.

"The ego sets goals to prove. The soul sets intentions to express. The ego is afraid to miss out. The soul only longs to become."

The Flame and the Mirror

He held up a small lamp, its flame flickering.

"This flame doesn't ask whether it burns brighter than another. It just burns. That is its nature. Your soul is like this flame. It is not meant to compete—it is meant to shine. But if you hold a mirror too close, all it will see is itself, distorted. Sometimes, our ambitions are just distorted reflections of who we think we should be."

Guruji turned once more to Apeksha and said, "To know if your dream is yours—feel how your body responds when you speak of it in solitude. If your heart softens, your spine straightens, and tears threaten gently without pain—that is your truth. That is your path."

Apeksha bowed her head—not in confusion, but in clarity. Not in burden, but in lightness. For now, she understood: the greatest success was not in reaching a goal, but in recognising the soul that called it forth.

Abhilasha's voice was gentle, but her question carried depth. 'Guruji,' she asked, 'what emotions arise when we visualise our desires—are they rooted in love, worthiness, and alignment, or in lack and urgency?'

Guruji looked at her with an expression—but the journey behind her question.

The Soil Beneath the Seed

"Abhilasha," he said, "imagine holding a seed of a beautiful tree in your hand—a tree you long to see bloom. Now imagine planting it in two different kinds of soil."

"One is soft, rich, and nourished with sunlight and love. The other is dry, cracked with urgency and fear of missing the growing season."

He paused and looked around the hall.

"Same seed. Different soil. But the tree that grows from love stretches upward, effortlessly, as if the sun itself is cheering. The one from fear may sprout—but it strains, bends, weakens… because it was not born from belief, but from pressure."

Guruji turned to Abhilasha.

"So too with your desires. What matters is not only what you visualise—but where that vision is rooted."

The Girl and the Empty Bowl

"Let me share something," he continued. "There was once a little girl who came to a temple with an empty bowl. Every day, she stood before the altar and prayed, 'Please fill my bowl. Please give me something.' Her voice trembled with desperation."

"Days passed. The priest noticed her and one morning asked gently, *Why is your bowl always empty?*'"

"She replied, *Because I need it to be filled.*'"

"The priest smiled and said, *No, child. Your bowl is empty because you bring it with emptiness in your heart. Try this instead—come tomorrow, not with a bowl of need, but with a heart of gratitude. See what changes.*"

"The next day, she came with no bowl at all. Just folded hands and a smile. And that morning, something magical happened—villagers began offering her sweets, a woman gave her a scarf, and the priest placed a lotus in her hand. She left with more than her hands could hold."

Guruji looked at Abhilasha, his eyes deep like still water.

"It was not the bowl that filled her life, but the energy she brought to it."

Emotions Are the Architects of Reality

He leaned slightly forward now, his voice carrying the rhythm of awakening.

"You see, the emotions you carry when you visualise your dreams are not just feelings—they are the *frequency* that shapes your reality."

"If your vision is soaked in lack—'I want this because I don't have enough'—then you are only amplifying that lack. You're standing in the hallway of abundance, shouting your emptiness."

"But if your desire is born from alignment—'I wish to expand because I already know I am worthy, whole, and ready to serve'—then you are already walking through the door of grace."

The Mirror of Self-Worth

"Desire is not the problem," Guruji said. "Desire is sacred. The real question is: *Do you believe you are worthy of receiving what you ask for?*"

Guruji paused.

"Most people don't struggle because they lack the dream. They struggle because they secretly believe they are not *enough* to receive it. That belief becomes a silent resistance."

He placed his hand gently on his chest.

"Before you ask the universe for something… ask your heart: *Am I asking from fear or from fullness? From lack or from love?* The answer to that will shape not only what comes to you—but who you become in the process."

The Wind and the Kite

Guruji said, "Desires are like kites. The wind is the universal force. But your emotions? They are the thread you hold. If your hand trembles with doubt, the kite dances wildly or crashes. But if your grip is steady with trust, the wind lifts your dream higher than you imagined."

He smiled, the kind of smile that lives at the edge of eternity.

"So ask yourself always—not just what you want, but *why* you want it… and who you are while asking."

Roopa, calm and thoughtful, gently raised her hand and asked, "Guruji, how vividly can we describe the life we wish to live? If our desires were a painting, how much of the canvas still remains blank?"

A hush fell. Her words didn't ripple through the air—they anchored. Guruji looked at her with the kind of stillness that could make even time hold its breath.

The Unpainted Portrait

Guruji began, "Roopa, your question is not a question—it is a mirror. And not everyone dares to look into such a mirror."

Guruji, after a pause, said, "Every desire you carry is a colour. Every thought you think is a stroke. Every action you take is the brush's rhythm. But most people stand before the canvas of life hesitant—afraid to begin, afraid to be bold, afraid to ruin what isn't even yet imagined."

He paused, letting the weight of that truth settle.

"Some people only sketch outlines—vague dreams of 'success,' 'love,' or 'peace,' without ever choosing the shades of how that love feels... how that peace breathes."

The Blind Artist

"There was once an artist who had gone blind in his youth," Guruji began. "He had once painted great murals—skies that seemed to breathe, rivers that shimmered with sunlight. But after losing his sight, he stopped painting."

"Years passed. Then one day, a child visited him and asked, *'What do you see when you close your eyes?'*"

"The artist replied, *'Everything. The sea. The stars. My mother's laugh. The texture of prayer.'*"

"The child smiled and said, *'Then why don't you paint again?'*"

"The old man sat in silence. That night, he picked up his brush again—not to replicate what he had seen, but to express what he remembered, what he *felt*."

"His next painting, they say, made people cry. Not because it was perfect—but because it was *true*."

Guruji turned to Roopa.

"It wasn't vision he needed. It was *clarity of heart*."

The Soul's Blueprint

He continued, "Roopa, many people say they want 'freedom,' but they never ask themselves: *What does freedom look like for me? Is it a mountain cabin? A morning without alarms? The joy of dancing in the rain?*"

"They say they want 'love'—but do not describe: *What kind of love? Gentle or passionate? Quiet understanding or poetic madness?*"

"They want 'success'—but whose version? The one they've seen on magazine covers, or the one where their heart sleeps peacefully at night?"

Guruji smiled gently.

"Until you dare to colour in your canvas, you're living someone else's painting. And often, it's not even complete—it's just borrowed outlines."

The Sculptor Within

"You are the painter," he said, his voice like river water flowing through sunlight. "But also, the paint. You are the sculptor—and the clay. When your desires are specific, vivid, and emotionally charged, they stop being distant stars and start becoming constellations guiding your steps."

He paused, letting the moment breathe.

"If your life were a painting… would it show movement or stillness? Colour or shadow? Would it echo your truth—or your conditioning?"

Then gently:

"If you don't dare to imagine your joy in detail, how can life conspire to deliver it?"

A Moment of Reflection

Buddha Hall was silent.

Roopa's eyes misted, not with sorrow—but recognition.

She whispered almost to herself, *"There are entire corners of my canvas I've never touched…"*

Guruji smiled, as if he had heard the whisper inside her heart.

"Then begin today," Guruji said. "Not with pressure—but with presence. Not to impress—but to *express*. Even a single brushstroke from the soul is worth more than a thousand borrowed masterpieces."

The fragrance of sandalwood still lingered in the air. As the conversation circled between souls and silences, Akanksh, with a contemplative calm, asked: "Guruji, what daily actions or rituals are helping us to hold our vision with consistency and presence?"

A gentle rustle passed through the drapes. Outside, a koel sang from somewhere deep in the trees. Guruji looked at Akanksh and spoke softly, like a sacred stream finding its path through stone.

The Lighthouse Within

"Akanksh," Guruji began, "a vision without grounding is like a lighthouse without a foundation—it may shine for a moment, but it cannot guide for long."

"Our dreams are not meant to be distant stars. They are seeds placed in the soil of our days, watered not by wishful thinking, but by **rituals of remembrance**—daily choices that reflect who we are becoming."

He leaned slightly forward, voice deepening with quiet fire.

"If your dream is the sun, your rituals are the orbit."

The Weaver's Thread

He turned slightly toward the gathering, eyes half-closed, as he recalled:

"There was once an old weaver in a Himalayan village. Each morning, before even the birds sang, she would light a small lamp, touch her loom, and whisper, *'May my hands remember my grandmother's rhythm.'* Only then would she begin her work."

"For years, her rugs looked ordinary. But one winter, a merchant came and saw something rare in her fabric. He asked, *'How did you create such beauty in the weave?'*"

"She smiled and said, *'The threads are nothing but my prayers, repeated in silence. Each line holds my breath from the morning, my stillness from the dawn.'*"

Guruji paused.

"She wasn't weaving cloth. She was weaving her presence."

The Invisible Practices That Build Visible Realities

He turned to Akanksh. "Every great vision must descend from the skies of imagination to the soil of practice. And that descent happens through sacred habits."

He then shared a few, not as rules, but as *anchors*:

- **Morning Silence**: "Begin with five minutes of stillness—where you are not chasing the dream, but holding it like a baby bird, gently, with wonder."

- **Daily Rehearsal**: "Visualise your future self—not just achieving—but being. Feel their calm, their energy, their choices. That vibration becomes your path."

- **Action in Alignment**: "Each day, do one small act in the direction of your vision—not to prove, but to move. A letter was written. A step taken. A truth spoken."

- **Evening Integration**: "Reflect not on what you lacked, but on what you *honoured* today. This changes your lens from lack to alignment."

The Garden and the Gardener

Guruji smiled, the corners of his eyes creasing like wisdom written in time.

"You ask, *'How do I hold my vision?'* But the truth, Akanksh, is—when your actions are consistent, your vision begins to hold *you*. Like a garden holds the gardener. It grows in response to your presence."

He folded his hands gently.

"Do not wait for motivation. Invite devotion. Let your rituals become a form of love—a slow dance between who you are, and who you are becoming."

The Flame That Never Fades

"Even the brightest flame dies without fuel," he said. "Our vision needs emotional oxygen. It needs the discipline of joy—not the discipline of pressure. Think of your rituals as love letters to your future self."

A few devotees had closed their eyes. Some were weeping silently—not from sorrow, but from something remembered.

Guruji looked around the hall, **"Do one thing daily that honours the life you wish to live. It doesn't have to be grand. Just consistent. Just honest. Just lit with intention. And slowly, that life will rise—not as a miracle, but as a mirror."**

CHAPTER III

Rule 2 – Positive Thinking

"Your mind listens to the words you plant. Speak with kindness—grow with care—and your life will bloom accordingly."

– Shree Shambav

Synopsis

Your mind is the garden where your reality takes root. Positive thinking is not about blind optimism or avoiding pain—it is about choosing thoughts that nourish your spirit rather than deplete it. In this chapter, we journey beyond surface-level motivation and explore the deeper power of reframing, gratitude, and self-affirmation.

By understanding the relationship between thought patterns and energy, you'll begin to recognise how your inner dialogue shapes the world around you. Through mantras that resonate with your truth and gratitude that ground your awareness in abundance, you'll learn to replace mental noise with conscious creation. Positivity, when anchored in authenticity, becomes a daily act of inner transformation.

Sujitha sat with quiet intensity, her hands gently clasped on her lap. Her eyes searched for something more than an answer—they sought a mirror to her mind.

She turned toward Guruji and asked softly, "What are the recurring thoughts that shape our inner dialogue, and how do they reflect our current self-image and worldview?"

A hush followed. Not the silence of emptiness—but the kind of stillness that precedes truth.

Guruji placed his hand gently on the armrest, closed his eyes for a moment, and then opened them—brighter, fuller.

"Sujitha," he began, "your question is the key to a hidden palace—the place where thoughts become thrones and beliefs, the kings."

The Sculptor and the Dust

"There was once a young sculptor," Guruji said, "She inherited her father's workshop, filled with marble blocks and unfinished statues. Among them was one block her father had never touched—covered in dust, cracked at the corners, long ignored. Everyone said it was flawed, worthless. But something in her paused before it every morning. Something called her to try."

"She began chiselling, little by little—removing only the dust at first, then clearing the cracks. And then, day by day, the figure of a radiant woman began to emerge. She wasn't creating something new. She was uncovering something that had always been there."

Guruji paused, letting the weight of the story settle into the hearts around him.

"Our thoughts," Guruji continued, "are like the chisel. Our recurring self-talk is the way we sculpt our inner statue. If every day you say to yourself, 'I'm not enough,' 'I'm too late,' or 'I can't,' then you are carving away your own worth with each stroke. Not because it is true—but because you've heard it too often."

The Echo Chamber and the Window

"Imagine," he said, "you're standing in a room of mirrors—every wall reflecting back your image. But the mirrors are cracked, dusty, and distorted. You begin to believe the image they show you. You forget that the cracks aren't yours. They are the filters of conditioning, wounds, societal noise."

"Now imagine one mirror shatters, and behind it is a window. Through it, light streams in. That window is awareness."

"Awareness of your recurring thoughts, your internalised beliefs—this is the first step to freedom.

You stop fighting the reflection and begin cleaning the glass."

The Deep Truth

"Our inner dialogue," Guruji said softly, "is often inherited. A child told they are too loud may grow into an adult who is afraid to speak. A young heart abandoned may grow into someone who questions their worth in every relationship."

"These thoughts become mantras—not the sacred kind, but the silent ones that limit us: 'No one listens to me.' 'I always get left behind.' 'Others are luckier.' These shape our choices, shrink our courage, and dim our light."

"But," he said, eyes glowing, "you can choose new mantras. You can re-script the narrative."

A Practice in Reflection

"Ask yourself, Sujitha," Guruji said, turning to her with gentleness, **"What sentence do you repeat to yourself most often in silence?"**

Is it one of trust or fear? Of expansion or limitation? Of love or doubt?

Because that sentence is a seed. And whatever you water will bloom—inside you, and around you."

Sujitha's eyes welled—not from sadness, but from sudden clarity. She nodded, slowly. She now knew that her inner voice was not a recording—it was a living breath, and she held the pen to write again.

Rohith's voice, steady but touched with vulnerability, pierced the silence.

"Guruji," he asked, *"when faced with challenge or loss, how do we consciously redirect our thoughts without invalidating our emotions?"*

Guruji looked at him with a gaze that didn't answer immediately but *held* the question, like cupped hands around a flickering flame.

The Weight of the Unspoken

Guruji leaned forward slightly. "Rohith, your question carries something very sacred. Not just about thought—but about the heart's need to be heard."

He paused.

"There's a river in Kashmir," he began. "It's called Lidder. Cold, clear, pure. One spring, a sudden landslide blocked its course. The villagers feared a flood, but the river… it didn't fight. It pooled for a while. It waited. Then, without force, it carved a new path—patiently, gently, without abandoning its source."

He looked around.

"That's how we must treat our emotions when grief or hardship visits. *We don't rush to reroute the river. We let it gather. We allow its presence. And only when it is acknowledged can it gently begin to flow again.*"

Emotions Are Guests, Not Dictators

"You see," Guruji said, his voice soft like silk brushing against stone, "our emotions are not enemies to be silenced or weaknesses to be corrected. They are sacred visitors—messengers. When we face a loss, a betrayal, or a wound, and we rush to 'think positively,' we often commit a silent violence against our own soul. We shut the door on the guest who only wanted to be seen."

"But maturity," he continued, "is not in indulging emotion endlessly nor in suppressing it. It is in *witnessing it fully—and then, gently, choosing what we feed with our focus.*"

The Broken Pot and the Blooming Path

"Let me tell you a story," Guruji offered.

"There was once a village woman who carried two clay pots every day from the river. One pot was cracked. It leaked. The other was whole. The cracked pot felt shame for its flaw, always delivering less water. One day it wept and said, 'Why do you still use me when I fail you every day?'

The woman smiled. 'Look at the path on your side. Do you see the wildflowers blooming there? I planted seeds, and your tears watered them each day.'"

Guruji paused, his words now soft and piercing. "Challenge and loss are cracks in us. But they don't mean we're broken beyond use. They mean something new is trying to bloom along the path of our pain."

The Art of Redirection

"Rohith," Guruji said gently, "redirecting our thoughts is not denial—it is *discernment*."

"When a storm comes, the tree doesn't deny the wind. It bends. It breathes. And after the storm, it chooses again where to grow."

"In the same way, when sorrow visits, you sit with it. You honour it. You speak to it kindly. You write your ache. You walk with it. And then—when your heart says 'I am heard'—you choose thoughts that build bridges, not walls."

The Practice: Three Questions

"When pain arrives," Guruji said, "sit with it and ask:

1. *What is this emotion trying to show me?*

2. *Can I allow this feeling without making it my identity?*

3. *What gentle thought can I hold today, even in the shadow of this?*

This isn't spiritual bypassing. This is **emotional alchemy**—the art of turning ache into awareness."

The room was silent, but not empty. It brimmed with quiet tears, softened hearts, and the sacred realisation that one could feel deeply *and* rise fully.

Rohith exhaled slowly, his eyes moist. Not because he had received an answer, but because he had *remembered* something truer than pain: presence.

Guruji looked at the gathering with a quiet smile.

"You are allowed to feel deeply and still choose your direction.

You are not here to suppress storms—you are here to sail through them with truth as your compass."

Nita, soft-voiced and sincere, asked: "Guruji, how has gratitude shifted our perception of daily life, even in moments when not everything is going our way?"

Guruji closed his eyes for a moment. When he opened them, there was no rush in his gaze. Only presence.

The Unseen Thread in the Fabric of Life

"Nita," Guruji began, "gratitude is not something we give *after* life blesses us. It is the way we *receive* life, even when it feels unwrapped, uncertain, or unwanted."

He looked up toward the sunlight filtering in.

"Gratitude doesn't fix the situation—it transforms the *seer*. It doesn't make life perfect—it makes life *perceivable in its wholeness*."

The Cracked Window and the Rain

Guruji gestured gently with his hand. "Imagine sitting in a room on a rainy day. There is a crack in the window, and water drips through. You could spend the day cursing the rain, the flaw in the window, or the wet floor. And your world becomes nothing but a complaint."

"But then," he said, voice calm, "you notice how the rain paints the glass with rivulets like a song. How it cools the heat of yesterday. You place a small bowl under the leak, and soon it's filled with water that nourishes your garden."

"That shift—from irritation to appreciation—is not the world changing. It is **you seeing more of it**."

The Story of the Widow's Lamp

"Years ago," Guruji continued, "I met a widow in Rameswaram. She lived in a small hut near the temple, had lost her husband young, and had no children. Life, from the outside, had not gone her way."

"But every evening, she lit a lamp and placed it near her window. She said, 'Even if no one comes, the lamp will remember that I chose light.'"

One day, I asked her, 'How do you remain joyful in your solitude?'

She said, 'Because I do not count what I've lost. I count what I've loved.'"

Guruji smiled softly. "She had turned her pain into prayer—not by forgetting her grief, but by illuminating it with gratitude."

Gratitude Is Not a Transaction

"Many people treat gratitude like a payment—they'll offer it only when something goes right. But true gratitude is not a transaction. It is a state of perception. It is the soul saying, *even this has something sacred to show me.*"

He paused and looked around.

"Gratitude doesn't deny the hurt, Nita. It simply says, *there's more to the story than the ache.*"

The Practice: The Eyes of Enough

Guruji offered a practice.

"Before you eat, whisper 'thank you' to the hands that grew your food. Before sleep, whisper 'thank you' to the day, even if it was imperfect. When you wake, whisper 'thank you' to breath, to body, to being alive."

"Gratitude, done daily, turns survival into *reverence*."

The Lens of Gratitude

"Gratitude," Guruji said, "is a lens. And through it, even the cracks in life let the light in."

He looked at Nita, his voice quieter now. *"And when you look at life through the lens of gratitude, you're not ignoring your struggles—you're expanding your soul to hold them with grace."*

The hall fell silent again—not with emptiness, but with remembrance. Around the hall, hearts softened. Some eyes welled up—not from sadness, but from that sacred ache of truth.

Nita bowed her head, her question now an answered prayer. And in that stillness, the world seemed a little fuller, a little more sacred, and life—though unchanged—suddenly glowed from within.

Lalitha, her voice both hesitant and curious, spoke from the heart:

"Guruji, are our affirmations rooted in who we truly are, or are they borrowed statements we don't yet believe?"

A quiet ripple passed through the hall. It was a question that stirred something deep—not just in others, but in themselves.

The Echo vs. the Voice

Guruji opened his eyes, the corners soft with compassion.

"Lalitha," he said gently, "what you've asked is like asking whether the echo belongs to the mountain or to the voice that spoke first."

He continued, "Many affirmations people recite today are echoes—borrowed words, copied mantras, viral phrases with no roots in their own soil. They sound beautiful, but if not anchored in inner truth, they become noise."

The Paper Flower and the Living Garden

He raised his hand slowly, as though holding something invisible. "A paper flower may look perfect. But it has no fragrance, no roots, no growth. It cannot bloom."

"An affirmation not felt is like that—it may decorate your mind for a moment, but it will not transform your reality."

He turned to the group and added, "But when your affirmation is born from your own heartache, your own longing, your own knowing—it becomes *alive*. Like a seed from your soul, it begins to grow."

The Story of the Girl with the Mirror

"I once met a young girl in Bengaluru," Guruji said, "who came to me crying. She said, 'Guruji, I've been saying "I love myself" every day for a year. But I still feel unworthy. It feels like I'm lying to myself.'"

"I didn't give her another affirmation. I gave her a mirror and asked her to sit with herself for an hour each day in silence. Just looking. No words."

"Days passed. One day, she came back with tears—not of sadness, but of recognition. 'Now,' she said, 'when I say I love myself… It's not because I want it to be true. It's because I see who I am.'"

Affirmation is not Magic. It is Marriage.

"Affirmations," Guruji explained, "are not spells to cast. They are **commitments to become**. They are not meant to fix you—they are meant to *introduce you* to who you already are, underneath the noise of fear."

He paused. "Before an affirmation becomes a statement of truth, it must pass through the furnace of discomfort, doubt, and resistance. That's when it's working—not when it feels easy, but when it challenges your old beliefs."

Practice: Planting a Real Affirmation

Guruji looked directly at Lalitha and said, "Take a journal. Ask yourself—not what affirmation sounds good—but what words make your heart rise, even if only a little. Even if they scare you."

"Your real affirmation," he said, "may tremble when you first speak it. That's okay. Because it's not performance. It's remembrance."

Truth Doesn't Need to Shout

He looked around the circle.

"You don't need a hundred affirmations. Just one, whispered in truth, lived in action, and watered daily with belief."

He closed his eyes and said softly, *"And when that affirmation comes not from your mouth but from your marrow, even the universe listens differently."*

Lalitha bowed her head, eyes brimming—not with answers, but with clarity.

Around her, others sat in silence, holding the space—not to repeat empty words, but to finally feel their own truth rise within.

Midday Reflections Under the Banyan:

The banyan tree stood like a silent witness, its great roots sprawling like the hands of time across the sacred earth of Shambav Hall. Clouds wandered lazily across the sky, casting moving shadows on the soft ground, and the breeze carried with it the scent of sandalwood and the gentle rustling of leaves. It was not just lunch that had nourished the devotees—it was something in the air, a deep stillness after the morning's truths.

Under this open sky and quiet wind, Kiran, Sam, Alice, Sofia, Bhavya, Aarna, Dev, and John sat in thoughtful clusters, their voices hushed, their hearts still vibrating with the echoes of Guruji's words. Soon, Nita, Lalitha, Rohith, Sujitha, and others wandered over, drawn not just by curiosity, but by a longing for continuity—spiritual digestion after physical nourishment.

Akshaya, ever sensitive, noticed a soft gleam in Apeksha's eyes.

"Would you share a story from one of the earlier retreats in Kumbhariyur?" he asked gently. "Something that still lingers in your heart?"

Apeksha gave a humble nod. Her voice rose gently, riding the air like a forgotten hymn.

"The Silent Well of Kumbhariyur"

"It was many years ago," Apeksha began, "in the early monsoon. The retreat in Kumbhariyur had drawn seekers from across the country—some hopeful, some sceptical, some simply tired of the noise of life."

"We had gathered near an ancient well—dry for years. Its cracked walls and echoing emptiness became a metaphor for many of us. Guruji had asked us a simple question on the second day of the retreat: *'Do you know what you've stopped believing in?'*"

Her eyes closed momentarily, returning to that moment.

"We all sat there, confused at first. Some mentioned faith, some hope, some mentioned their own dreams. Then Guruji said something I will never forget: *'It is not the loss of water that dries a well. It is the silence of those who once drew from it.'*"

She paused, letting the silence settle.

"We realised—belief is not a thing we lose. It is a thing we stop drawing from. We stop visiting the well, and we call it empty."

The group under the banyan listened as though the wind itself had stilled to hear.

"One of the young seekers there, a boy named Aarav, had come carrying the guilt of failing his family business. He had labelled himself 'useless.' But that evening, by the firelight, he told Guruji, *'I don't believe I have anything worth giving anymore.'*"

"And Guruji smiled—not to mock, but to melt the ice. He said, *'Then give from your nothingness. Give presence. Give breath. Give silence. Even the empty well gives an echo.'*"

"By the end of the retreat," Apeksha said, her voice trembling just slightly, "Aarav stood beside that very well and offered the group a poem he'd written—his first ever. It wasn't perfect. It wasn't polished. But it was pure. And we all drank from it like water in the desert."

As the story ended, a cool gust swept the group, and Bhavya whispered, "What became of him?"

Apeksha smiled. "He now teaches poetry to underprivileged children. He says that we'll never emptied again."

Just then, Kiran sighed softly, looking at the sky that had begun to shift gently from grey to gold.

"It's time," he said, the words reverent. "Guruji will begin the afternoon session soon."

But none of them stood immediately. They sat a little longer, not out of lethargy but longing—to absorb, to remember, to draw just a little more from the well.

Because sometimes, a story isn't a story.

It is water.

And under that ancient banyan tree, hearts had quietly, wordlessly, begun to drink.

CHAPTER IV

Rule 3 – Emotional Alignment

"The universe does not respond to your words—it responds to the emotional tone beneath them."

– Shree Shambav

Synopsis

Manifestation is not just about what you want—it's about what you feel. Your emotions are the invisible language of your soul, the vibrational signals that shape your external reality. In this chapter, we explore the powerful concept of emotional alignment—the art of bringing your desires and feelings into resonance.

Through the cultivation of emotional intelligence, you begin to understand your emotional triggers, reactions, and the stories beneath them. You'll learn how to shift your emotional state not by repression, but through conscious awareness, mindfulness, and meditative practices that connect you back to your centre. When your heart and mind speak the same language, the universe listens more clearly.

The Paradox of the Hidden Tide: When Emotions Sabotage Desire

The Buddha Hall was quieter now. The afternoon sun filtered softly through the high windows, casting golden pools of light on the stone floor. The scent of jasmine still lingered faintly, a remnant of the garlands offered that morning. The devotees had gathered again—hearts stilled, eyes softened by the stillness of the midday reflections.

John raised his hand gently and asked, "Guruji, how often do our emotions support our desires, and when do they unconsciously contradict them?"

A deep quiet spread. Even the breeze at the edge of the curtain seemed to pause.

Guruji looked at him, his eyes not just seeing, but *feeling*.
He responded not immediately with words, but with a silence that drew the question inward.

The River Beneath the River

"John," Guruji said, "imagine a great river flowing toward the ocean. This river is your desire—strong, wide, filled with dreams and clarity. But underneath, beneath the visible current, is an *undercurrent*—your emotions. And if that undercurrent flows in the *opposite direction*, it slows the river's journey. Sometimes, it pulls it backward."

He paused, his fingers softly curling around his japa beads.

"Our minds may declare *'I want love'* or *'I want success,'* but if the undercurrent of emotion says *'I'm not worthy of love'* or *'I fear failure more than I desire success,'* the river meets resistance—sometimes subtle, sometimes devastating."

Guruji turned to the devotees, letting the depth of his metaphor land. Then he spoke again, this time softer.

"There was a young woman once, Rhea," he said, "who came to a retreat just like this. She had a vision board full of dreams—travel, healing work, a soulful partnership. Every word she spoke was of freedom and joy. But her energy..."

Guruji held his palm to his chest.

"...her energy trembled. She was not aligned with what she claimed to desire. I asked her to close her eyes and visualise her life five years into her dream. She did. And then, tears streamed down her face."

'Why are you crying?' he had asked her.

She whispered, *'Because I don't believe I deserve it.'*

And there it was—a river fighting its own undercurrent.

Guruji continued, "John, this is what I call *emotional dissonance*. The heart and the head are at war. The desire and the emotion are out of sync. And in that inner misalignment, manifestations stall."

"Your emotions," he said, raising a hand as if holding the invisible thread of truth, "are not just echoes of the past. They are co-creators of your future."

"So, what must we do?" he asked, answering his own question.

"We must become honest observers of our emotional language. Not just what we desire, but what we **feel** about that desire."

"Ask yourself: *Do I feel joyful or anxious when I visualise it?*

Do I feel expanded or contracted?

Is this born of love… or fear disguised as ambition?"

"Until your emotions vibrate at the same frequency as your dreams, you are pulling a chariot forward with one hand and tying it to a rock with the other."

The Sacred Reconciliation

A hush followed, one not born of silence but *absorption*. Many in the hall now looked inward. Old beliefs surfaced like forgotten letters in dusty drawers.

Then Guruji smiled—gently, knowingly.

"To manifest is not to force. It is to *harmonise*.

To feel worthy of the dream you hold.

To feel safe in the joy you seek.

To trust, not only in the destination, but in your right to arrive."

John bowed his head, deeply moved.

The Buddha Hall breathed with a sacred knowing, as though every being present had just been handed a mirror—and in it, they saw the river, the undercurrent, and the choice to flow in unity.

The clouds outside Buddha Hall had thickened into a silver hush. The breeze moved through the bamboo chimes that hung near the verandah, each note whispering something ancient. Inside, the devotees were still recovering from the depth of the previous reflections. The air felt sacred, like a pause between heartbeats.

Aarna, her eyes wide with innocence yet framed by the maturity of inner questioning, leaned slightly forward and asked: "Guruji, what are the dominant emotional states we live in, and how do they influence the energy we project daily?"

Guruji, seated in the subtle golden light pouring through the lattice, closed his eyes briefly—as if listening not just to the question, but to the space behind it.

Then he opened his eyes and began, voice gentle, but clear:

The Climate You Carry

"Every one of us," Guruji began, "lives in a personal atmosphere. Just as the earth has its weather, we too carry an emotional climate—some carry sunlight, others thunder, some carry winds of restlessness, others the still waters of grace."

He smiled.

"This emotional climate is what you project, often without realising. It enters the room before your words do. It wraps itself around your relationships, your choices, your creativity, your success… and yes, even your spiritual path."

The Story of Tarun and the Forgotten Garden

Guruji leaned slightly forward, "I remember a young man from years ago—Tarun. He was bright, brilliant even. Wanted to start a centre for healing, something noble. But every time he tried, something collapsed. Not outside, but *inside*. He would get anxious, easily frustrated, and doubt his ability. He asked me once, 'Why does nothing flow for me?'"

"I asked him to keep a journal—not of what he *did* each day, but what he *felt*. For three weeks."

Guruji's eyes softened. "He returned with pages full of hidden storms. Resentment. Self-doubt. Impatience. Fear."

"Guruji, I didn't even know I felt all this," he said to me, teary-eyed.

"And that was the beginning of his freedom—not a new plan, not more effort, but a shift in emotional awareness. He had unknowingly planted his garden with seeds of resistance and wondered why nothing blossomed."

Your Emotions Are Not Private

"Emotions are not silent whispers within you," Guruji continued. "They are the *songs the universe hears first*. You may say, 'I want peace,' but if you live in a state of irritation, what you project is conflict."

"If you carry grief long enough, even your laughter carries a tremble. If you live in gratitude, your very presence becomes healing—even in silence."

He turned toward Aarna now, eyes filled with kindness.

"The question is not just: *What do I feel?* The deeper question is:

What feeling am I rehearsing so often that it has become the background music of my life?"

The Mirror and the Magnet

"Your dominant emotional state is a magnet," Guruji said. "It doesn't just reflect your life—it shapes it."

"Imagine your inner state like a mirror. If it's fogged with fear, you see a distorted world. If it's clean with clarity, the world reflects your light. What you feel consistently becomes what you attract."

He paused, letting that truth sink in.

"We often try to fix life at the *symptom level*—changing jobs, partners, goals. But the true transformation happens when we shift our baseline emotional frequency. From scarcity to sufficiency. From anger to understanding. From anxiety to trust."

The Gentle Challenge

"Every morning, ask yourself," Guruji said softly:

- *'What emotional state do I live in without question?'*
- *'Does this feeling help me rise, or does it quietly sabotage my becoming?'*

"Then gently, patiently, begin the rewiring—not through suppression, but through presence."

"Choose gratitude over complaint. Choose compassion over judgment. Choose peace over urgency. Not once. But over and over. Until the climate changes. Until your life starts blooming in ways that finally feel like home."

Aarna's eyes shimmered. A few others lowered their heads in reflection. The room felt full, not with sound, but with **self-realisation**.

Outside, the clouds finally gave way to a gentle drizzle. And inside Buddha Hall, hearts quietly turned toward their own inner weather—ready, perhaps for the first time, to change the season from within.

The drizzle had stopped. The earth outside Buddha Hall exhaled the rich scent of softened mud and fallen neem leaves. The wind stilled, almost as if the world had leaned closer to listen.

Dev's voice broke the silence—not rushed, not loud, but heavy with the weight of a question he had likely carried for a long time. "Guruji, how do we typically respond to discomfort—do we avoid, suppress, or sit with it in conscious presence?"

The Unopened Letter

"Discomfort," Guruji said, "is the soul's handwritten letter. But most of us treat it like spam."

He looked around the room slowly.

"Have you ever received a letter from someone you didn't want to hear from? You tuck it away, burn it, distract yourself. But the message waits. And it grows heavier not because of what's written inside, but because of your resistance to read it."

"Discomfort is that unopened message—from pain, from truth, from memory, from transformation."

The Three Roads

"There are three common ways people deal with discomfort," Guruji continued, now walking slowly before the seated devotees.

'Avoid.'
"We run from it. We distract ourselves—scrolling endlessly, chasing newness, silencing stillness with sound. But unprocessed pain doesn't vanish. It gets stored—in the body, in the nervous system, in the

decisions we unconsciously make. Avoidance is the slowest poison."

'Suppress.'

"Suppression is more subtle. You say: *I'm fine. It's nothing. I've moved on.* But emotions are not guests that leave when ignored. They turn into shadows—resentment, chronic tension, unexplained sadness. What you suppress doesn't disappear—it disguises."

'Sit With It.'

"To sit with discomfort is a sacred act. It means you face the wound without turning away. You allow the tremble, the grief, the shame, without labelling it 'bad' or 'wrong.' And in doing so, you discover: the pain is not the enemy—your resistance to it is."

The Story of the Crying Child

Guruji's tone softened into a story.

"Once in the village of Kumbhariyur, during a retreat, a little girl wandered into our space. She was crying—not loudly, just this quiet, aching sob. Her mother tried to hush her, pulling her away."

"I asked her to bring the child to me. I held her—not with the goal to stop the crying, but simply to be there. I didn't ask why. I didn't offer sweets. I didn't distract her with toys. I just stayed present."

"She cried for a few more minutes… then stopped. And fell asleep in my lap."

Guruji looked at Dev now.

"Sometimes, your discomfort is like that child. It doesn't need to be fixed. Just held. Just witnessed. And when it feels safe, it will release itself."

The Fire and the Flame

He continued, "Discomfort is not a punishment. It's a passage. It's the fire that burns away the false—illusions, roles, and masks. But if you flee the fire, you flee the gold it reveals."

"You are not the discomfort," Guruji said. "You are the awareness that can *hold* it without being consumed."

Dev's Realisation

Dev's eyes moistened. He had been running—from a heartbreak, from a failure he hadn't named, from a part of himself he hadn't dared to meet. And now, in the stillness of Buddha Hall, the running had stopped.

He whispered, "Then presence is the balm?"

Guruji nodded. "Presence is not the absence of pain. It is the loving witness to pain. And when pain is witnessed fully—it transforms."

"Next time discomfort visits you," Guruji said, "invite it to tea. Let it sit beside you. Ask it what it has come to show. And above all, don't rush it away. Because the very thing you are trying to avoid may hold the key to who you are becoming."

The banyan tree outside rustled softly. Inside, hearts stirred—not with answers, but with permission. Permission to feel. Permission to stay.

The devotees bowed—not just to Guruji, but to the discomforts they would now meet, not with fear, but with presence.

After a long moment of thoughtful silence, Bhavya spoke, her voice calm but weighted with vulnerability: "Guruji, what practices help us realign with peace, joy, or clarity when we feel emotionally uncentered?"

Guruji, after a pause, said, "Such a beautiful question. And such an important one. Because everyone feels uncentered. The difference is—some stay lost in the fog, and others learn to return."

Guruji's eyes softened, his voice a gentle current.

"Many years ago, in the forests near Kumbhariyur, there was a stream that ran through a path where I often walked. Every morning, I'd cross it, and I noticed something peculiar—right in the middle of the stream lay a large stone. It never moved. Day after day, season after season, the stream danced around it."

He paused, letting the quiet take over before continuing.

"One winter morning, after a storm, the water had risen and was gushing with power. The stone was still there. But this time, I noticed fine moss growing on its back—soft, green, untouched by the fury around it. And it struck me."

"The stone didn't fight the stream. It didn't complain about the cold waters or shifting tides. It simply *remained*—anchored. And because of that stillness, life began to grow upon it. It became a resting place for birds, a quiet spot where sunlight danced."

Guruji turned to Bhavya.

"That stone reminded me of what we all forget: you don't have to control the stream to find peace. You only have to be *present* in it. When emotions surge like a flooded river, don't swim against them. Anchor inward. Let your breath be the moss. Let your silence be the stone."

He paused, then added with weight, "The stream never stopped flowing. But because the stone stayed, it created a sacred centre. That's what realignment is.

You don't push the water away—you become the sanctuary within it."

The Compass Within: Three Anchors of Realignment

Guruji continued:

1. Stillness as Medicine

"In moments of chaos, the first practice is stillness—not to escape emotion, but to feel it fully without judgment. Sit. Close your eyes. Let the storm speak. Most emotional turbulence arises not from the feeling itself, but from our resistance to it."

He looked at Bhavya.

"Stillness is not passivity. It is the most courageous act of listening."

2. Breath as a Bridge

"The breath is the only part of the body not bound by time. The past cannot touch it. The future cannot claim it. The breath is now. When we feel scattered, we must return to this invisible ally."

He raised his hand.

"Breathe slowly, with presence. Inhale: I am here. Exhale: I release. Do this ten times. Your nervous system will remember what your mind forgot—that peace was never lost. Just buried."

3. Movement as Memory

"When words don't work, when the heart feels heavy—walk. Dance. Stretch. Movement brings the body back into rhythm. Emotions are energies in motion. Let them move, and they'll move *through* you."

The Kumbhariyur Practice

Guruji then turned his gaze toward Apeksha, who nodded knowingly.

"In one of our retreats in Kumbhariyur, a young man came to me. He had lost his job and his sense of self. His face was hollow with despair. I didn't give him a lecture. I gave him a bowl of grains and asked him to feed the temple birds each morning."

"Every day, he'd arrive with hunched shoulders. And slowly, day by day, he started smiling again. One morning, he said, 'Guruji, the birds were never waiting for food. They were waiting to feed *me* something else.'"

Guruji's eyes softened.

"Sometimes, small acts of beauty restore our own forgotten worth."

Bhavya's Reflection

Bhavya whispered, "So… the return to peace is not a grand gesture?"

Guruji nodded.

"It's a gentle turning. A moment of attention. A ritual of remembrance. Your peace never leaves. It waits behind your noise."

He gestured to the group.

"Create rituals, each of you. Light a lamp at dawn. Chant a verse at dusk. Walk barefoot on the earth. Keep a journal of small joys. These are not habits—they are soul anchors."

The Wind Carries the Lesson

Outside, the wind picked up again, soft and sure. And it felt to everyone present as if it were carrying Guruji's words through the banyan, into the soil, into the bones of the earth itself.

"Bhavya," Guruji said gently, "don't wait for perfect peace. Offer your presence to the moment—and peace will arrive like a faithful friend who never truly left."

PART TWO

The Journey Within

Releasing, Realigning, and Reclaiming

"Inspired action doesn't shout—it whispers through the soul. Ego demands speed, but intuition invites grace."

-Shree Shambav

CHAPTER V

Rule 4 – Taking Inspired Action

"Inspired action doesn't shout—it whispers through the soul. Ego demands speed, but intuition invites grace."

- Shree Shambav

Synopsis

True manifestation is not about hustle—it's about harmony. Taking action toward your goals is essential, but the quality of that action determines the outcome. Inspired action is born not from stress or obligation, but from a soul-level clarity that feels energising, not exhausting.

This chapter explores the key difference between ego-driven effort—often rooted in fear, comparison, or urgency—and soul-led action that flows from alignment, intuition, and trust. Inspired action may look small on the outside but carries immense momentum because it's in sync with your highest self.

You'll learn how to recognise intuitive nudges, overcome the illusion of procrastination, and build consistent, meaningful momentum without burnout. When action arises from love instead of lack, it becomes a sacred expression of faith in your vision.

Sofia asked, "Guruji, what inner signals help us distinguish between action led by fear or pressure versus action inspired by inner alignment?"

Guruji began, gently, "Sofia, imagine standing at the edge of a dense forest. There are two paths ahead—both winding, both unknown. One path is crowded with voices outside you—urging, demanding, judging. The other is silent… but your heartbeat feels steady when you look that way, even if it's unfamiliar."

"That," Guruji said, "is the difference between fear-driven action and soul-aligned action."

The Story of the Two Drummers

"Let me share a story," he continued. "Once, in a mountain village, there lived two drummers—Ravi and Veer. Both were invited to play at the king's annual festival. Ravi, wanting to impress, began to practice day and night. But his rhythm came from a place of anxiety. 'What if I'm not good enough? What if Veer outshines me?' he worried. Each beat he played was tight, tense, rushed—an echo of his unrest."

"Veer, on the other hand, would rise each morning, sit by the river, and listen. Not just to the water, but to the rhythm within himself. Then, he'd drum—slowly at first, then with heart. His hands danced with joy, not pressure."

"When the day of the festival arrived, Ravi's performance was technically perfect, but lacked soul. Veer's, however, made even the trees seem to sway. The villagers wept, laughed, and danced—not because of skill, but because of *sincerity*."

The Pulse of Alignment

Guruji leaned forward slightly, as if letting the teaching land directly in each listener's chest.

"The inner signals of alignment are subtle—but unmistakable. They come not with noise, but with *knowing*. Aligned action feels spacious, not rushed. It may still come with fear—but the fear is not the leader, it is the passenger. The driver is presence."

"When you're driven by fear, your body contracts— your breath shortens, your decisions come from urgency or a need to prove. But when you're aligned, even hard work feels meaningful. There is an ease beneath the effort. Your body, your emotions, and your intuition are in quiet agreement—even if the outcome is uncertain."

He closed his eyes for a breath, then said: "So the question to ask is not 'Should I act?' but *'From where within me is this action arising?'* Is it from panic, or from presence? Is it a reaction… or a response rooted in clarity?"

A soft breeze entered Buddha Hall as if nature itself had exhaled in agreement. Sofia bowed her head slowly, a tear balancing in her lashes—not from confusion, but from recognition.

And in that quiet, everyone reflected not just on the question, but on their *why*, their *where*, and their *what next*.

Alice asked, "Guruji, can we recall a time when we followed a soul-nudge instead of a logical plan? What was the result, and how did it feel?"

Guruji closed his eyes for a moment, as if reaching into a memory that lived not just in his mind but in the very fabric of his being. Then he opened them and began, softly.

The Soul's Detour

Guruji leaned back slightly in his seat. "There was a young man," Guruji began, "a seeker, like many of you. He lived in Chennai, working a steady job, living a life most would call respectable. But inside, he felt a strange emptiness—a longing without a name. One day, stirred by a deep yearning for meaning, he decided to leave everything behind and travel north to Rishikesh, hoping to find answers in the land of saints."

"He packed lightly. His train was at sunrise. His mind was made up. But sometimes, the soul has plans beyond what the mind can comprehend."

The Man at the Edge

"As he waited on the platform, minutes before departure, he noticed an old man sitting barefoot near a pillar. He wasn't begging. He wasn't even watching the crowd. Just sitting. Still. Silent. His presence was like a stone in the river—solid, unmoved."

"Something in the seeker stirred. A quiet voice inside whispered, *'Go sit with him.'* It made no sense. The train was moments away. His entire future was arranged around this journey. But the nudge wouldn't let go."

The Abandoned Ticket

"He obeyed. He walked over, sat beside the old man. For a long time, they didn't speak. The train came and went. The seeker never looked back."

"Eventually, the old man opened his eyes, glanced at him, and said only this: *'Sometimes, the silence inside you knows the way long before your feet do. Listen to that.'* And then he stood and walked away."

"The young man stayed in Chennai. Days later, while volunteering at a meditation centre, he met the teacher who became his inner compass. His path didn't lead to the mountains. It led inward."

When the Map Folds Itself

Guruji let the story settle into the stillness of the hall.

"Not every calling is dramatic. Some arrive like whispers in the noise. But when followed, they carry the power to rearrange a life."

He looked around slowly.

"We are so often taught to chase what's planned. But sometimes the soul rewrites the itinerary. Not to confuse you—but to align you."

"The real compass is not logic. It is *presence*. A nudge that bypasses strategy and awakens knowing. And when you say yes to it—you don't lose time. You *merge* with it."

He turned to Alice, his voice now layered with reverence.

"Logic builds ladders. But soul-nudges open doors you didn't even know existed. They don't always lead to comfort, but they always lead to truth."

The Signature of the Soul

He paused and then asked the gathering, "Do you know how it feels when you follow such a nudge? It's not free of fear. But there is a quiet certainty that hums underneath the fear. Your heart expands. Time slows. And even if no one else understands… *you* do."

"A soul-nudge often comes disguised as an irrational impulse—a call to leave the familiar, speak without rehearsing, say yes before you're ready. It doesn't argue. It invites."

Guruji smiled gently.

"The mind asks, *'Will this work?'* But the soul whispers, *'This is yours.'* And when we follow it, the outcome is rarely what we expect—but almost always what we need."

There was stillness in the Hall again—not heavy, but sacred. A few looked inward, replaying their own moments of unexplainable courage, silent detours, and blessings born from intuition.

Alice folded her hands, her question now transformed into understanding.

And outside, the breeze carried a whisper, as if the world too had once followed a nudge… and became sky.

The Shadow Behind the Delay

Sam leaned forward, voice steady yet curious. "Guruji, in what ways does procrastination show up in our life, and what might it be trying to protect us from?"

"Procrastination," Guruji began, "is rarely a sign of laziness. It is a veil—a hesitation between the self we are and the self we are afraid to become."

He continued, his tone woven with story.

The Tale of the Unfinished Poem

"There was once a boy named Varun, a gifted poet from a small coastal town. His words had the power to move hearts, and his teacher often said he was born with ink in his veins. He was working on a poem that was meant to be his finest—one that spoke of love, death, and the soul's journey through sorrow. But days passed. Then weeks. And the poem remained unfinished."

"His friends accused him of being lazy. But what they didn't know—what even *he* didn't fully understand—was that every time he approached the poem, a deep fear rose within him. *What if it's not as good as they expect? What if I pour all of me into it, and it still isn't enough?"*

"So he delayed. Distracted. Pretended it didn't matter."

The Fear Beneath the Surface

"Procrastination," Guruji said gently, "often hides not laziness but *fear*. Fear of failure. Fear of being seen. Fear of our own greatness. And sometimes, fear of the changes that success might bring. We do not delay because we are weak—we delay because we sense transformation lurking at the edge of the task."

He paused, then added: "Sometimes we'd rather stay in the safety of the familiar than step into the fire of becoming."

The Protective Self

"Sam," Guruji looked at him now, "Procrastination is often the inner child pulling the adult hand back from the flame. It is protection dressed as postponement. And instead of scolding it, we must *listen to it*. Ask it, 'What are you afraid will happen if I begin?'"

Rewriting the Inner Contract

Guruji leaned slightly forward. "To move beyond procrastination, we don't just need motivation. We need healing. We must create safety within—where it is okay to try, to fail, to be seen, and to rise again."

Guruji smiled, then said: "Varun did eventually finish his poem. Not because he conquered fear. But because he sat with it. He allowed the trembling. And the trembling became a part of the poetry."

"Each time we procrastinate," Guruji said, "let us not ask, *'Why am I not doing this?'* Instead, let us ask, *'What part of me is afraid, and how can I offer it love before I move forward?'* Then the resistance melts—not through force, but through kindness."

The Lightest Step That Moves Mountains

A gentle drizzle tapped against the roof of Buddha Hall. The air was hushed, infused with the scent of jasmine and sandalwood, while within the circle of seekers, a quiet yearning shimmered—unspoken, yet felt.

Kiran, always reflective, raised his voice like a prayer carried on the wind. **"Guruji, what small, joy-filled step can we take today that feels light, clear, and aligned with our larger purpose?"**

Guruji turned to him with a soft smile, the kind that cradled both question and questioner.

The Sparrow's Thread

"In a forest once parched by drought," Guruji began, "a fire broke out. It spread rapidly, swallowing trees, nests, and all that breathed beneath the canopy. As the larger animals fled in fear, a tiny sparrow darted to and from a nearby stream, carrying droplets of water in her beak."

"'Foolish bird,' the eagle scoffed. 'You think you can put out the fire with those drops?'"

The sparrow didn't stop.

"I may not quench the whole fire," she chirped, "but **this is my part**. My drop may not save the forest, but it saves my soul from standing still in helplessness."

Guruji paused.

"Purpose," he said slowly, "does not always roar. Sometimes it flutters. Sometimes it whispers. Sometimes it is a sparrow carrying hope."

The Myth of Monumental

"We often believe that our purpose must be grand," he said, his voice like soft rain on dry earth. "That, unless the step is massive, it's not worthy. But in truth, destiny responds not to scale, but to **sincerity**."

He turned to the group and asked, "Have you ever seen a seed hesitate because it cannot become a forest in one day?"

Silence answered.

"A smile to a stranger, a page written in silence, five mindful breaths before replying in anger, one honest conversation with yourself—these are not small things. They are signals. Beacons. Threads of light that weave a future aligned with your essence."

From Delay to Dance

Guruji looked at Kiran. "When the step you take carries joy, it becomes a prayer. When it is rooted in lightness, it becomes sustainable. And when it aligns with your heart, it becomes magnetic."

He closed his eyes for a moment.

"Imagine a dancer performing not for the stage, not for the applause, but because the movement itself is devotion. Let every step you take toward your purpose feel like that. A dance—not a duty."

Guruji opened his eyes, now reflecting the calm of a mountain lake.

"So today, Kiran," he said gently, "perhaps you do not need to climb the peak. Perhaps all you need is to put on your walking shoes with a smile. That single act, done with joy, has already changed your trajectory."

Evening Under the Banyan Tree

The air was thick with silence—not the absence of sound, but the kind that arrives when nature prepares to sleep. The wind had turned cooler, brushing against the dampened earth like a whisper. Birds had settled into their nests, their songs now replaced by the gentle rustle of leaves. Above, the sky wore a robe of deep indigo, its fabric stitched with faint stars barely peeking through.

After the day's intense sessions, **Guruji** softly instructed, "Let's take a short evening break. Let the teachings settle like dew."

The devotees slowly made their way to the old banyan tree—a sacred witness to many unspoken revelations. Akshaya, Padma, Vasudeva, Kiran, Vidyarthi, Aastha, and Abhirami were the first to arrive. Soon, Nita, Lalitha, Rohith, and Sujitha joined them, forming a quiet circle of presence.

The hush was gentle. The earth, slightly wet from a brief drizzle earlier, smelled of memory.

Then, Padma, her shawl wrapped tightly around her shoulders, broke the stillness.

"Let me share something," she said softly, her voice carrying both warmth and weight. She turned to Apeksha, who was now seated close by. "Do you remember...?" she asked.

Apeksha gave a small nod, her eyes already glimmering with what she knew was coming.

The Story of the Last Candle

Padma began, "It was three years ago, during a winter retreat in the hills near Kodaikanal. The place was secluded—just a few of us and Guruji. The power had gone out that evening, and the retreat hall was lit with nothing but candles. The temperature was biting, and the silence outside was deep enough to hear your own heartbeat."

"We were in the middle of a session on surrender, and Guruji had just posed a question: *What is the light you carry when everything around you grows dark?*"

Padma paused. The wind rustled a few dry leaves overhead. No one moved.

"That night," she continued, "one by one, the candles started flickering out. There were about ten of them. Eventually, only one candle remained on the altar. Its flame danced wildly with the wind coming through the old windows."

"I remember being fixated on that last flame. So small. So fragile. But it kept burning. We all sat watching it in silence—maybe for minutes, maybe for an hour. Time blurred."

"And then," her voice thickened, "it went out."

She closed her eyes, breathing in slowly.

"It was so still… none of us spoke. But in that darkness, something extraordinary happened. I realised that my fear of the dark was gone. That night, for the first time, I didn't need the flame outside to remember the flame within."

Tears in the Darkness

When Padma opened her eyes again, many others had theirs closed—faces turned inward, tears quietly trailing down.

"No one said much the next morning," she said. "But we all walked lighter. As if something invisible had been lifted."

She looked around at the gathered souls.

"I share this now because sometimes, you think your light is too small to matter. Too weak to survive the storm. But even a fragile flame has purpose. Even a brief light can teach the soul to remember its eternal fire."

Silence wrapped them like a blanket. Abhirami reached for Aastha's hand. Sujitha wiped a silent tear.

Then Kiran let out a quiet sigh, almost a whisper, "It's time for the next session…"

But no one rose immediately.

Because in that moment, under the soft rustle of the ancient banyan, something had already begun—the next session was not a teaching, but a remembering.

CHAPTER VI

Rule 5 – Letting Go of Resistance

"Resistance is the tension before the release—when you surrender, the storm within settles and clarity emerges."

– Shree Shambav

Synopsis

Manifestation flows when resistance dissolves. This chapter dives deep into the practical and emotional work needed to identify, face, and release the mental blocks that silently stall your progress. Resistance often hides in limiting beliefs, fears, and the illusion of control. Learning to surrender doesn't mean giving up—it means trusting the unseen currents of life and allowing space for the universe's wisdom to unfold.

You'll explore powerful techniques to gently unbind yourself from old patterns, cultivate faith in the timing and process, and practice detachment without losing your passion or vision. True letting go is an act of courage, opening you to receive with an open heart and clear mind.

Martina asked, "Guruji, what recurring thoughts or beliefs create invisible barriers that hold us back from manifesting our desires?"

The Wall That Wasn't There

"Many years ago," Guruji began, "a traveller arrived at a distant village known for its sacred gardens and wise elders. But as he approached, he saw a towering stone wall surrounding the village. There was no gate. No ladder. No passage. Just the wall."

"The traveller sat before it, disheartened. Every day, he would walk along its length, trying to find an opening. He tried climbing it. Tried calling over it. Days passed. Then weeks. Eventually, he gave up. He made a small camp by the wall and lived outside, never entering the village he had dreamed of reaching."

Guruji paused, his voice like a soft wind stirring memory.

"Years later, a child from the village wandered near the outer edge. The traveller called out and told her of the wall—how he had longed to cross it but couldn't. The child looked puzzled. She stepped forward, and with a small hand, touched the stone."

'What wall?' she asked. 'There's nothing here.'

"The traveller rose, disbelieving. He reached out. And to his shock... his hand passed through. The wall wasn't made of stone—it was made of fear."

The Architecture of the Mind

Guruji turned to Martina now, his tone tender.

"You see... the strongest walls we ever face are rarely made of matter. They are built from belief. From thoughts repeated so often, they harden into invisible architecture."

He began to name them softly, as though unveiling ghosts.

"I'm not ready. I'm not worthy. I always fail. Others have it easier. I'll do it tomorrow. What if they laugh? What if I lose it again?"

"These thoughts," he continued, "aren't just passing clouds. They become the mortar in the walls we live behind. We decorate these walls with logic, hang curtains of reason, and forget that we ever built them ourselves."

The Sacred Demolition

Martina's eyes were wide, moist.

"So how do we break them, Guruji?" she asked.

He smiled, a smile that knew storms and sunlight alike.

"You don't need to break what was never real. You need to *see* it."

He leaned forward slightly. "The moment you become aware that a belief is just a thought you've said yes to—again and again—you loosen its grip. And the more you act from your *vision* rather than your *vibration of fear*, the less real the wall becomes."

"Some walls crumble in one act of courage. Others need daily whispers of truth: *I am enough. I am ready. I am allowed to shine.*"

He looked around the room now, his gaze sweeping across silent faces.

"Freedom," he said, "begins when we question the thoughts we've mistaken for facts. When we stop asking if we're good enough, and start remembering that we were born from light itself."

Martina closed her eyes for a moment, not to escape—but to see more clearly. And for the first time, she noticed something:

The wall she had lived beside for years… was no longer solid.

It had been only a shadow, waiting for the sun of awareness to dissolve it.

Kieron asked, "Guruji, how do we experience surrender—is it a feeling of loss, trust, or something else—and how might embracing surrender shift our manifestation process?"

Guruji simply closed his eyes for a moment, then opened them with the softness of someone who has walked through fire and returned with water.

The Boat in the Storm

"There was once a young sailor," Guruji said, "who had never left the calm lagoons of his coastal village. But something within him longed for more—new lands, open skies, a taste of the unknown."

"So one day, with blessings from his elders, he set sail in a modest wooden boat. The sea welcomed him at first—soft waves, stars guiding him, wind like a hymn. But as he ventured deeper, a violent storm arose."

"Lightning tore across the sky. Waves towered like mountains. The young sailor did all he was taught— pulled the ropes, tried to steer, shouted prayers into the thunder. But the more he tried to control the boat, the more it spun wildly."

"He collapsed, exhausted, thinking it was the end."

Guruji's voice dropped to a hush. "But then, something strange happened. In that moment of collapse—not despair, but *surrender*—he let go. Not of the boat, but of the need to fight the storm. He tied himself to the mast, folded his hands, and whispered, 'I trust the sea.'"

"The storm didn't end instantly. But something inside him did—the resistance. The fear. The illusion of control. And in that release, the boat began to flow *with* the current, not against it. By morning, the storm had passed. And the sailor found himself near an island he never charted—but later called home."

The Hidden Power of Surrender

Guruji turned gently to Kieron.

"You asked what surrender feels like. Many think it's a defeat—a giving up. But true surrender is not collapse; it is a *rise*—into trust."

He continued, voice like a river finding its course:

"Surrender is not the end of desire. It's the beginning of alignment. It's saying, *I still want this—but I no longer grip it with fear. I let life flow toward it through me, not only from me.*"

He gestured softly toward the gathering.

"So many people try to manifest with their fists clenched—affirming goals with urgency, visualising with strain. But manifestation is not just an act of will; it is also an act of *allowing*."

"When you surrender," he said, "you stop planting seeds and digging them up every day to see if they've grown. You trust the soil. You trust the sun. You trust *yourself*."

The Sacred Shift

Kieron was quiet, his breath deeper now.

"Is surrender a loss?" Guruji echoed his question softly. "Perhaps. But only the loss of illusion. Of the belief that you must do it all alone, control every ripple."

He smiled, almost playfully.

"The wind carries farther when the sail is open—not when it's forced. Surrender isn't stepping away from the dream. It's stepping out of the way."

Astyn asked, "Guruji, what are practical ways we can detach from the outcome without detaching from our vision or passion?"

The Archer and the Wind

"There was once a young archer in a Himalayan village," Guruji said, "who trained for years to perfect his aim. Day after day, he would tie his hair back, line up the bow, and shoot at a single tree bark from increasingly greater distances."

"One day, the king's envoy announced a grand archery competition. The reward was not just gold, but the honour of becoming the royal archer. The young man's heart surged—he knew he had skill. But the thought of winning began to infect his practice."

"He would grip the bow tighter. Sweat would gather before he drew the string. His hand would tremble—not from fatigue, but from *attachment* to the outcome."

Guruji's voice slowed.

"And so, he began missing. Not because he lacked mastery, but because he was no longer *present*. He wasn't shooting to release the arrow—he was shooting to *capture a result*."

The Lesson in the Leaves

"One morning," Guruji continued, "he sat alone under a Bodhi tree near the riverbank. He watched a dry leaf twirling gently to the ground. It landed softly, without force, without aim. And in that moment, something shifted in him."

"He returned to the field, this time holding the bow like a prayer, not a weapon. He breathed, not to impress the judges, but to become *one* with the arrow's flight. When he released it, he smiled—regardless of where it landed."

"And that day, not only did he win, but he said later: *'I learned that mastery is not about controlling the target. It's about loving the flight.'*"

Practical Detachment: Loving the Flight

Guruji turned to Astyn, his gaze filled with kindness.

"To detach from the outcome is not to become indifferent," he said. "It is to love your vision so deeply that you no longer tie your worth to how it unfolds."

He raised his palm.

"Do your work like the sun shines—fully, generously, without needing applause. Let your passion burn like a lamp in the night, not for the sake of who will see it, but because it is your nature to shine."

He offered three practical ways to embody this balance:

1. Anchor in the *Why*, Not the *When*

"When your desire is rooted in meaning, not in timeline, it stays sacred. Ask yourself, 'Why does this matter to my soul?'—not just 'When will it happen?'"

2. Celebrate Progress, Not Just Peaks

"Honour the little alignments: the insight you gained today, the person you became in the process. Outcomes are chapters. But who you become—that's the book."

3. Practice the Sacred Pause

"Each day, take a few minutes to *visualise without grasping*—feel your dream, then release it into the river of trust. Let it go like a feather, knowing the current knows its path."

Guruji said gently, "Detachment is not the absence of desire. It is the presence of trust. You hold your vision with open hands, not clenched fists—so it can rise, not suffocate."

Astyn's eyes softened. The others, too, sat quietly—hearts stirred by the reminder that **manifestation is not only what you build, but how you *be* while building it.**

Espen asked, "Guruji, how can trust in the timing and flow of the universe help us move through moments of doubt or impatience?"

The Story of the Mountain Seed

"There was once a farmer in the foothills of the Nilgiris," Guruji began. "He received a rare seed—unlike any he had ever seen. The elder who gave it to him whispered, *'This will not grow like the others. It will test your faith before it bears its gift.'*"

"The farmer, curious and hopeful, planted the seed in a corner of his field. Days passed. Then weeks. Other seeds sprouted, flowered, and fruited. But this one—remained still. His neighbours laughed. Even he began to doubt."

"But each day, he watered it. Spoke to it. Sometimes even sang to the soil. Not because he was sure—but because he chose *faith over certainty.*"

Guruji paused and glanced up at the dark velvet sky.

"Six months later, just after the first thunderstorm of monsoon, a tiny green shoot emerged. Not like the others—it was stronger, slower, and strangely radiant."

The Bamboo Within Us

"What he didn't know," Guruji said, "was that he had planted a Himalayan bamboo. For months it grows not upward, but *downward*, building a complex root system—anchoring, preparing, deepening."

"And when it finally begins to rise, it shoots up *ten feet in a week*. But only because its roots were quietly preparing the miracle."

He turned toward Espen now, voice gentler, more intimate.

"Doubt and impatience come when we judge growth only by what we see. But the soul, like that bamboo, often grows *invisible roots* in times of stillness."

The Dance of Divine Timing

"To trust the universe," Guruji continued, "is to believe that there is intelligence in the pause, wisdom in the delay, and unseen grace even in silence."

"Sometimes your manifestation needs you to *become* ready for it—your emotional landscape, your energetic capacity, your alignment. The universe is not punishing you with time; it is preparing you with love."

He added with a smile, "A baby born too soon needs an incubator. So do our dreams."

How to Cultivate That Trust

Guruji then offered Espen and the others three ways to deepen this sacred trust:

1. Return to the River

"Go to nature. Watch how rivers don't rush—yet reach the ocean. Trees don't force their bloom—but still flower. Let their rhythm become your teacher."

2. Trust What's Quiet

"When nothing seems to be happening outside, know something sacred is shifting within. Use that season to align your thoughts, refine your beliefs, and deepen your presence."

3. Make Waiting a Ritual, Not a Void

"Waiting isn't passive. It's devotional. Light a candle. Breathe into your heart. Say to yourself: *I am willing. I am becoming. I am trusting.* That, my child, is not waiting. That is preparing."

The Sacred Space Between Desiring and Receiving

A soft silence followed. No one moved—not because they were afraid to break it, but because they were soaking in it.

Guruji then said, "Impatience is the ego's doubt in the soul's timing. But trust... trust is the music of the universe playing softly beneath your fear. When you listen, you'll find the rhythm again."

Espen bowed his head, heart loosened, burden lightened. Around him, others breathed a little deeper, as if something unseen had finally unclenched.

CHAPTER VII

Rule 6 – The Power of Belief

"What you truly believe in your heart and subconscious mind creates the blueprint for your reality."

– Shree Shambav

Synopsis

Belief is the invisible architect of your reality. This chapter explores how strengthening your belief in yourself and your ability to manifest rewires the subconscious mind, transforming doubt into unwavering confidence. Your beliefs shape not only your thoughts but also the energetic field you project—directly influencing the outcomes you attract.

Through practical tools and inspiring success stories, you'll learn how to identify limiting beliefs, replace them with empowering truths, and cultivate emotional self-belief that fuels consistent manifestation. Reprogramming your subconscious is a journey of love, patience, and persistence, unlocking the full power of your creative potential.

John asked, "Guruji, what limiting beliefs about ourself and our abilities have we internalised, and how do they affect our manifestation results?"

Guruji closed his eyes for a moment, breathing deeply, as if gathering not words, but truth from the silence.

Then he opened his eyes, voice gentle—yet full of weight.

The Unseen Soil

Guruji said, "Imagine you are a gardener. You sow seeds of mangoes, roses, lilies—dreams of joy, abundance, creativity. You water them with action, you place them under sunlight with intention… yet, nothing grows."

"Why?"

He let the question hang in the air like incense.

"It is because the **soil beneath** is full of stones you never saw. Old roots you never cleared. Shadows that never belonged to you, yet still live there."

"Our **limiting beliefs**," he explained, "are not usually loud. They don't announce themselves with drama. They hide—quietly—underneath the very things we want."

The Quiet Prison

"There was once a boy in a village," Guruji began, "who was told from the time he could speak, 'You must be careful. You are weak. Don't dream too big, or you'll fall harder. Stay humble. Play small. You're not like the others.'"

"He never questioned it. Why would he? The voices came from those he loved. So, he grew into a man who smiled on the outside but doubted on the inside. He spoke of wanting freedom, but chose cages dressed as comfort. He wanted to sing—but believed his voice was too soft."

"And every time life gave him a chance to rise, some unseen thread held him down. That thread… was not fate. It was a *belief*."

The Mirror That Lies

"You see," Guruji said, "many of us are living not by truth, but by **reflections we believed were truth**—childhood comparisons, early failures, an insult we heard when we were vulnerable, a moment of shame when no one stood for us."

"These beliefs become laws in the subconscious:

'I'm not smart enough.'

'Love isn't for people like me.'

'If I try, I'll fail.'

'Others get lucky, not me.'"

"And the worst part?" he paused.

"We **don't even know** we believe them."

The Dull Knife

"Imagine trying to carve a beautiful sculpture with a dull knife," Guruji said. "You'll say, 'I have the vision, I have the desire, but it's not working.' And you will blame the stone. Or time. Or karma. But in truth, your *tool*—your **belief**—was never sharp enough."

"You cannot manifest gold from a furnace that only believes it produces rust."

The Unlearning Begins

"But here is the grace," Guruji whispered. "Beliefs are not carved in stone. They are etched in smoke. And you—yes, you—have the match to burn them away."

"It begins with noticing," he said softly. "Notice the thought behind the hesitation. Notice what you tell yourself when something good begins to come. Ask: *'What story am I carrying that no longer belongs to me?' 'Whose voice am I still obeying in my silence?'"*

He continued, "Transformation does not come only through goals. It comes through **unlearning**."

The Real Practice

"If you wish to manifest joy, then you must believe you are worthy of joy. If you desire abundance, but your root belief is scarcity, then you will always sabotage the very door you try to open."

"Until the inner voice says:

'I am enough, not because I achieved. But because I am.'

Until then, manifestation will remain a beautiful concept, but not a lived truth."

Guruji looked around, his eyes glowing with something ancient. "We must become gentle torchbearers of our own minds. Not angry. Not rushed. But curious. Ask yourself each day:

What would a person who loved themselves truly believe right now?
And then… begin to believe that."

"Because your **outer life** will only ever rise to meet the **inner story** you whisper to yourself when no one else is listening."

Silence fell again.

But this time, it was not empty.

It was full—like rainclouds ready to pour.

Tears welled up in a few eyes. Not from sadness.

But from recognition.

Each devotee sat quietly, holding their unseen stone. And some, for the first time, began to feel the courage to release it.

Dev asked, "Guruji, how do we currently nurture or undermine our self-confidence, and what changes can strengthen our inner belief system?"

Guruji looked at Dev—his eyes resting not only on the question, but on the space from which it had risen.

He did not answer immediately. Instead, he reached for a small lamp placed beside him and held it up gently.

The Flame Within the Wind

"This lamp," Guruji said, "has only a little flame. But see how it burns—soft yet steady. What keeps it alive is not just the oil, but the quiet protection around it."

"Our self-confidence," he said, "is just like this flame. It begins as something tender. It needs nurturing, shielding from harsh winds, and feeding through presence. If exposed too early to stormy doubts or criticism, it flickers... and sometimes goes out."

"Many of us grew up with people who did not know how to protect that inner flame. Not out of malice, but out of their own wounds. So, we internalised voices like:
'You're not good enough.'

'That's not for you.'

'Don't dream so big.'"

"These voices became our **inner narration**, and without knowing, we now relight our flame, only to **blow it out again with our own breath**."

The Story of the Paper Boat

Guruji leaned forward, the story unfolding like a sacred scroll.

"There was once a little boy who loved to build paper boats. One day, he built one so beautifully, he felt sure it would float far down the stream. He ran to the village brook and released it."

"But the boat barely moved—it sank before reaching even the first bend."

"The boy was disappointed, and when the villagers mocked him, he never made another boat."

"Years passed. He became a man with great ideas—but he never acted on them. Whenever something new stirred in him, a quiet voice said, *What's the point? It will sink anyway.*"

"The problem wasn't in his skills," Guruji said. "It was in that old story—a belief formed in childhood that had never been challenged."

How We Undermine Ourselves

Guruji paused, letting the story soak in, then added with gentle clarity:

"We undermine our confidence when we:

- Dwell on past mistakes instead of learning from them.

- Compare our journey with another's and shrink.

- Use negative self-talk in the name of 'being realistic'.

- Surround ourselves with voices that echo doubt instead of truth.

- Wait for external validation before giving ourselves permission to try."

"And each time we do this," he continued, "we **signal to the soul** that we do not trust its worth."

Strengthening Our Inner Root

"But," Guruji said, eyes glinting with compassion, "confidence is not gifted by fate. It is **grown like a tree**—with daily watering and gentle pruning."

"To strengthen your inner belief system, you must:

- Celebrate even the smallest of wins.

- Speak to yourself like someone you deeply love.

- Honour your word to yourself, even in tiny promises.

- Dare to act *before* you feel fully ready.

- Keep the company of those who reflect back your light, not just your shadows."

The Story of the Mountain Path

"I once met a shepherd in the hills of Himachal," Guruji recalled. "He was leading a goat up a steep path. I asked him, 'How does she climb this steep cliff with such ease?'"

"He smiled and said, 'She's not thinking of the top. She only places her foot on the next stone.'"

"That," Guruji said, "is the way of true self-confidence. It's not about leaping to the peak. It's about trusting your next step—over and over—until one day you look up, and realise… you've become the mountain."

The Sacred Refrain

He closed his eyes and whispered more than spoke:

"If you want to believe in yourself again, stop asking, *'Will I succeed?'*

Instead, ask, *'Can I honour myself enough to try, without shaming myself if I fall?'*"

"Self-confidence," Guruji concluded, "is not loud. It's not about ego. It's a quiet contract between your soul and your breath, signed each time you choose growth over fear, presence over perfection, and love over doubt."

Dev's eyes glistened.

And in the quiet that followed, many in the hall realised—perhaps for the first time—that their flame had not gone out.

It had only been waiting...

for them to breathe with it

rather than against it.

Aarna asked, "Guruji, how can we recall a personal or observed success story where belief directly influenced the outcome? What lessons can we draw from it?"

The night had grown silent under the starlit canopy. The banyan leaves shimmered softly as the breeze whispered through. The earth held a calming stillness, as if awaiting a truth that needed to be heard.

Guruji looked at Aarna with warmth in his eyes.

But instead of answering right away, he simply said, *"Let me tell you a story... not of a sage, nor a warrior—but of a weaver named Sakshi."*

The Weaver and the Loom of Dreams

In a quiet village nestled between hills and rice fields, lived a woman named Sakshi. She was known for her modest hut and her handwoven sarees—each thread dyed with natural colours, each pattern inspired by temple bells, monsoon skies, and stories told under lantern light.

But what most didn't know was that Sakshi carried a dream much larger than her loom.

She wished to open a school—not just for literacy, but for **dreaming**. She wanted to teach children not just letters, but courage. Not just arithmetic, but belief. In a village where most girls were married by sixteen, and boys left school to work in the fields, her dream felt impossible.

They laughed at her.

"Sakshi," they said, "you are a weaver. That is your place. Dreams like yours are for city people, or the rich."

But Sakshi would smile. She never argued. She only whispered to herself, *"Belief is the first thread. Without it, the loom cannot move."*

The Invisible Thread of Belief

Every day, she would weave for hours—selling sarees, saving every coin. At night, she would sketch her dream on scraps of old paper—desks made of bamboo, shelves of books, the laughter of children echoing in mud-walled rooms.

It took five years.

But one day, with nothing more than her saved money, her inner fire, and a borrowed shed, Sakshi opened her school. Only seven children came in the first week. But she taught them with love and wonder. Word spread. Within a year, she had forty students. By the third year, donors began to visit. The shed grew into a building. The building into a campus. And today—**it stands as a place where hundreds of children learn not only subjects, but the power of possibility.**

When Sakshi was once asked how she managed this feat with no support, no formal education, and no initial backing, she simply said:

"They all waited for proof.

I only needed belief."

The Lesson in the Threads

Guruji turned to the group, voice soft but powerful:

"Belief is the unseen architect behind every reality.

Not the loud kind of belief that shouts to the world,

but the quiet one that shows up each day despite the world."

Sakshi's story is not unique in spirit. It lives in every mother who believes her sick child will recover. Every artist who paints a canvas that no one has yet seen. Every soul who walks a dark path, trusting that dawn will come.

The Seed in the Stone

"Belief," Guruji said, "is like a seed placed between rocks. The world may say it won't sprout. But if that seed believes in light, it will find even the narrowest crack… and grow toward it."

"Many people wait to believe until they see results. But the irony is—the results wait for belief before they can appear."

Turning Inward

Then, addressing Aarna directly, Guruji asked gently, "Now, tell me… was there ever a moment in your life when something unfolded beautifully—not because you were certain it would, but because you chose to believe in it anyway?"

Aarna paused, her breath catching.

She thought of the time she had applied for a scholarship she felt underqualified for, and how despite the odds, she'd trusted her essay and her heart. And how, against logic, she had won.

She nodded slowly, tears misting her eyes.

Guruji smiled.

"The universe is not asking for your perfection, child.

It is only asking for your participation.

And belief… is how we say yes."

Bhavya, her voice soft but resolute, leaned forward and asked, "Guruji, what daily practices can we implement to consistently reprogram our subconscious mind toward positive, empowering beliefs?"

The Garden Beneath the Surface

"Bhavya," Guruji began, "the subconscious mind is like a garden buried just beneath the visible ground of our awareness. It does not speak in language, but in symbols. It does not argue, but absorbs. And whatever seeds you plant in that hidden soil—whether weeds of fear or roots of strength—it will grow them quietly, persistently."

"You see," Guruji continued, "most people try to change their life by trimming the leaves above—fixing habits, making resolutions, saying mantras once or twice. But lasting change comes not from the leaves… it comes from the soil."

The Music Box and the Mind

"There was once a boy named Arvind," Guruji began. "He was gifted a beautiful music box by his grandfather. But over the years, it stopped playing clearly. The melodies were broken. He opened the box, changed the crank, and polished the outside—but the song still stuttered."

"Finally, a watchmaker told him, 'You must open the mechanism deep inside. The problem isn't in the tune, it's in the program that plays it.'"

Guruji paused.

"And so it is with us. If our daily experience is full of fear, doubt, or self-sabotage, the issue isn't our outer behaviour—it's the old recording playing beneath it."

Rewriting the Inner Script: Practical Practices

Guruji turned toward Bhavya with gentle firmness.

"Here are five daily practices—simple, but powerful—that work like slow but certain chisels on the stone of the subconscious:"

1. Morning Visualisation (5–10 minutes)

"The subconscious is most receptive in the morning. Before touching your phone or the world, close your eyes. Imagine your desired life—clearly, emotionally, with full presence. Not as a wish, but as a felt experience. Smell the air, hear the sounds, become the you who has already become."

2. Affirmation with Emotion

"Don't repeat dry words like a parrot. Affirm with feeling. Say: 'I am safe. I am worthy. I am creating a life of beauty.' And say it until even the cells in your skin begin to listen."

3. Self-Observation Journal

"Each night, write what patterns repeated today. What thoughts kept surfacing? What triggered you? This simple act of witnessing makes the invisible visible—and what we see, we can transform."

4. Inner Dialogue Correction

"Throughout the day, catch your inner critic. If you hear, 'I always mess up,' replace it—gently—with, 'I am learning. I am growing.' The mind will resist, but over time, it will surrender to kindness."

5. Sleep Reprogramming

"As you fall asleep, whisper affirmations like lullabies. Your subconscious never sleeps. Feed it with faith before the world's noise returns."

Analogy: The River and the Rocks

Guruji leaned forward and said,

"Changing the subconscious is like redirecting a river. You cannot do it by yelling at the water. You do it by placing one stone… each day… with care and consistency. At first, the river flows the same way. But one day—it turns."

"And so will you," he said, looking at Bhavya. "You are not trying to force change. You are teaching your soil to grow new roots."

The Final Truth

"Every belief that holds you back was once a whisper repeated in fear. Now, choose whispers of power. Speak them daily. Not because you are lying to yourself—but because you are finally telling yourself the truth."

A hush followed.

The wind rustled through the banyan leaves, as if the trees themselves were nodding.

CHAPTER VIII

Rule 7 – Cultivating Patience and Persistence

"Patience is not the absence of action but the presence of faith in the unseen rhythm of life."

– Shree Shambav

Synopsis

Manifestation unfolds in its own divine timing, and cultivating patience is the spiritual art of trusting that process. This chapter reveals the alchemy of time—the way persistence works hand in hand with patience to transform waiting into growth. Delays and setbacks are not failures but sacred invitations to deepen your resilience and expand your mindset.

You'll learn how to develop a growth mindset that embraces challenges as lessons, stay committed to your vision even when results seem distant, and discover practical strategies to sustain your motivation. Patience is not passive waiting; it is active trust coupled with steady, inspired action.

Alice asked, "Guruji, How do we currently experience waiting or delays in our manifestation journey, and what emotions typically arise during these periods?"

Guruji looked at Alice with a quiet, knowing gaze, then gently closed his eyes for a moment. When he opened his eyes, there was the weight of lived experience in his voice.

"Alice," he said gently, "have you ever watched the sky before a storm?"

"She nodded slowly."

"There's a stillness," he continued. "The clouds gather. The wind shifts. The birds fly lower. Nature prepares. But to the untrained eye, it looks like nothing is happening. It's quiet. It's slow. It's uncertain. Yet beneath that silence, forces are aligning—subtle, powerful, invisible."

The Sky Before the Storm

"There was once a young boy named Rivan in a coastal village who dreamed of becoming a sailor. Every day he would run to the edge of the sea, building his little raft, watching ships pass, reading the stars, speaking to the horizon as if it were listening."

"But for years, no opportunity came. His family was poor. His town had no port. Everyone laughed at his dream, and slowly, doubt crept in. One day, in despair, he threw his maps into the fire and declared, 'The sea doesn't want me.'"

"But that night, a storm came unlike any seen in decades. It tore through the coastline and stranded a foreign vessel on the nearby rocks. Rivan, knowing the tide and currents by heart, was the only one who could navigate the rescue. And in that act—what he thought was a failed dream became the doorway."

"He wasn't waiting," Guruji said, "he was unknowingly preparing."

Waiting is Weathering

"We often mistake quiet seasons for failure. But waiting is not absence. It is presence in a deeper rhythm. It is like the ocean—calm on the surface, but full of currents that cannot be seen. When we wait with resistance, we drown in our own impatience. But when we wait with attention, with surrender, we begin to notice how life moves in spirals, not straight lines."

The Question Beneath the Waiting

"Ask yourself," Guruji said, "what kind of watcher are you during your waiting? Do you fill the space with fear, or with faith? Do you panic when your vision delays, or do you tend to your inner weather—your thoughts, your moods, your trust?"

He paused, letting the air itself carry the weight of the question.

"Because the truth is… it is not just about what you're waiting for. It's about who you become in the waiting."

The night air wrapped around them like a shawl. The wind had quieted, but something deeper had awakened within the hearts of those gathered.

Alice's eyes shimmered. "So it's not lost time. It's layered time."

Guruji smiled. "Yes. Sometimes the universe is not denying your desire—it's sculpting the shape of your readiness."

A Story from the Village of Kumbhariyur

Guruji leaned back and told a story.

"Years ago, during a silent retreat in Kumbhariyur, there was a young woman named Nancy. She had a powerful vision—to open a school for underprivileged girls in her village. Every day, she wrote affirmations, prayed, planned, and visualised it. But year after year, nothing seemed to move.

Government approvals were denied. Sponsors withdrew. The land she was promised was sold to someone else. And slowly, the vision she once held with fire became a whisper in her heart."

"One evening, she sat beside me under the same banyan tree and said, 'Guruji, I think the universe isn't listening.'"

I asked her, 'Is that true—or are you expecting the universe to deliver your order like a waiter, not realising it's still cooking something far deeper?'

"She wept that evening, not from frustration—but from the release of her attachment. Something shifted. She stopped pushing. She started trusting. And she began teaching girls under the Jackfruit tree in her backyard with no building, no support—just presence."

"Two years later, someone who had once visited her class anonymously donated land and funding. That school now stands—not because she waited passively, but because she waited consciously, with love, not resentment."

Reflections from the Stillness

Guruji continued: "When we wait with expectation but no embodiment, we feel restlessness. We measure time like enemies of life. But when we wait with presence and alignment, we turn waiting into womb-space—a sacred container where the next version of us is quietly forming."

"Ask not just 'When will it come?' but also, 'Who am I becoming while I wait?' Because life will always give you more of who you are than what you ask for."

"Consider a seed in the soil," he said. "If you dig it up every day to check its progress, you'll kill it. But if you water it daily, protect it from harsh winds, and trust the sun—you'll one day sit in its shade. Waiting is not passive. It is a sacred collaboration with timing."

Alice whispered, "So we're not really waiting for life to move… we're learning how to stay still without falling apart."

Guruji smiled. "Exactly. Sometimes the greatest manifestation is learning how to hold yourself with grace, even when the world has yet to mirror your vision."

Sam asked, "Guruji, in what ways can adopting a growth mindset help us reframe setbacks as opportunities instead of viewing them as obstacles?"

The Story of the Sculptor and the Cracked Stone

"Let me tell you a story, Sam," Guruji began, his voice tender. "In the hills of Ellora, many years ago, lived a sculptor named Rajan. He was known far and wide for his ability to breathe life into stone. Kings sought him, temples were built by his hands, and yet—he remained humble, always saying, 'I am only discovering what is already inside the stone.'"

"One day, he received a commission to sculpt a deity for a sacred shrine. A perfect block of marble was brought to him from afar. But just as he began carving, a hidden crack surfaced—long and jagged. The villagers panicked. 'Throw it away,' they said. 'Get a new one.' But Rajan did not."

"He sat with the stone for days. Then he smiled. 'This crack,' he said, 'is not a flaw. It's a whisper. The sculpture is asking to be shaped differently.'"

Guruji paused.

The Sacred Crack: Reframing Setbacks

"What Rajan created," Guruji continued, "was not the deity originally planned. He carved a different form—one that leaned gently with the crack, that held it like a scar that spoke of survival. And that statue… became more beloved than the others. People said they could feel the compassion in its eyes."

"Sam, setbacks are cracks in the path—but they are not dead ends. They are redirections. Invitations. They're how life humbles us, reshapes us, and deepens the art of who we are becoming."

The Growth Mindset as a Mirror

"A fixed mindset says: 'I have failed. I am broken. This is the end.'

A growth mindset whispers: 'Something is being revealed. Let me listen.'"

Guruji leaned forward, his voice gentler now.

"Setbacks challenge the ego, not the soul. The ego wants to prove; the soul wants to grow. When you learn to look at a failure and ask, *What is this here to teach me?*', you are no longer defeated. You are transformed."

The Light in the Debris

"There's an old saying," Guruji said, "The seed does not weep when the shell breaks. It pushes through. The shell had to crack for the life within to emerge. Your obstacles are not blocks on your path; they *are* the path—rough, real, revealing."

"Resilience is not about becoming hard," he said. "It's about becoming *clear*—learning to see that life doesn't break you. It unmasks you."

Sam sat still, his eyes glistening. He wasn't just thinking—he was remembering. The moment of rejection that almost broke him. The project that failed. The quiet pain he never told anyone. And now, it all felt... repurposed.

He nodded slowly, "So the setback is the sculptor."

Guruji smiled, "And the growth mindset is the surrender that lets the chisel strike—not as punishment, but as poetry in motion."

The Sacred Rituals of Becoming"

The scent of jasmine lingered in the air. Outside, the wind whispered through neem leaves, and the occasional hoot of an owl punctuated the stillness.

Everyone sat in silence, wrapped in shawls, breath in sync with the hush that lives between words.

Kiran's voice rose from that silence, gentle but uncertain.

"Guruji, what practices or rituals help us maintain motivation and commitment when the manifestation feels slow or uncertain?"

Guruji didn't answer right away. He closed his eyes. Then, opening them slowly, he began—not with explanation, but with a story.

The Farmer of the Forgotten Valley

"In a remote valley where clouds rarely wept and the winds often forgot to carry hope, lived an old farmer named Bhairav. For years, he planted seeds in parched soil. Each morning, before even the birds stirred, he would step barefoot into his field, light a small lamp, and say aloud to the earth:

'I am here. I believe in you.'"

"His neighbours mocked him. *'The sky doesn't hear you,'* they said. But he never stopped. He watered the soil with his tears when water ran dry. He sang lullabies to the seeds. He made his life a ritual—not for results, but as a quiet offering to unseen forces."

Guruji's voice deepened. "And then… in the sixth year, the monsoon came. It didn't just rain—it *poured*. But only Bhairav's fields flourished. Because only Bhairav had stayed."

Devotion as a Daily Thread

Guruji turned slightly, his eyes scanning the candle-lit hall.

"When the fruit of our vision is delayed, our mind wavers. Doubt becomes loud. But devotion—true devotion—is not about receiving quickly. It's about becoming someone *ready* to receive."

He raised his hand gently, as though touching the idea mid-air.

"Your rituals are not about controlling time. They're about aligning with it. When the world is slow to reflect your effort, that's when your inner commitment matters most."

Rituals that Anchor the Soul

He offered gentle practices, each like a pearl dropped into still water:

- **Daily Alignment Check-In:** Sit in stillness and ask, *"Does this action match the frequency of the future I desire?"*

- **Symbolic Anchors:** Light a lamp, wear a sacred thread, touch the earth—something small but consistent, something your soul recognises.

- **Journal the Becoming:** Not just what you've done, but *who you're becoming* because of your devotion.

- **Micro-Celebrations:** Celebrate the internal victories—choosing hope over fear, love over doubt, trust over control.

"These are not chores," Guruji said softly. "These are sacred whispers to the universe. They say, *'I have not forgotten. I am still tending.'*"

The Sacred Wait

He closed his eyes for a moment, then opened them again with great tenderness.

"Bhairav once told his son, *'The rain was not my reward. My reward was becoming someone who never left the field.'*"

Silence followed—deep, holy silence. A few eyes glistened. Not from sadness, but from the aching beauty of recognition.

Guruji looked to Kiran, then to each one gathered in the Buddha Hall.

"When manifestation feels far, remember—your practice, your presence, your rituals are not delays. They are preparation. They are the language through which the unseen begins to trust you back."

"Make your life a ritual of remembrance. And even in the silence, the universe begins to bend."

Abhirami, usually quiet, raised her voice gently: "Guruji, how can we balance patience with persistence—knowing when to keep going, and when to surrender or adjust our approach?"

Guruji looked at her with deep affection, as if seeing both the question and the one who had carried it for long. He closed his eyes, drawing inward, then spoke not with haste, but with reverence.

The Story of the Sand Piper and the Sea

"Long ago, on the southern coast, there lived a sand piper—a small bird, delicate yet determined. One day, as she flew over the shore, she saw the sea carry away one of her eggs. The ocean had swallowed what she held most dear.

"She wept. She screamed. But no one came. And so, this tiny bird—fragile as a whisper—began to do the unthinkable."

"She walked to the edge of the shore, dipped her beak into the sea, and began pulling out water—drop by drop."

The devotees smiled gently, recognising the futility and the devotion.

"The other birds laughed. *'You are too small,'* they said. *'You will die before the sea notices.'* But she didn't stop."

"Day after day, she returned. Her persistence was not anger—it was love. Her patience was not resignation—it was trust."

Guruji paused, the silence returning like an old friend.

"After seven days, the winds changed. The sea stirred. And the Ocean Spirit, moved by her unwavering heart, returned the egg—placing it gently on the sand."

The Dance Between Patience and Persistence

Guruji turned toward Abhirami.

"Patience is not doing nothing. It is still faith that the seed will bloom—even if you cannot see the roots growing. Persistence is the quiet action—the tending, the trusting, the whisper that says, *'Just one more step.'*"

"But knowing when to continue and when to adjust… that comes from listening—not to fear, but to alignment."

Guruji raised his hand slightly, gesturing toward the heart.

"Sometimes, we push because of ego. Sometimes, we surrender because of exhaustion. But the wise learn to ask—*Is this action rooted in love or in fear? In alignment or in escape?"*

The Bamboo & The River Stone

Guruji smiled and continued.

"There is a difference between the bamboo and the river stone. The bamboo waits, builds, and holds steady roots in silence. But the river stone is persistent, shaped by water, letting go without resistance—yet it remains, beautiful, rounded, grounded."

"We are called to be both—bamboo in our still faith, and stone in our gentle endurance."

Practical Insight

Guruji offered practical reflection to anchor the story:

- **Ask yourself regularly**: *Is my persistence aligned with my joy, or am I holding onto something out of fear of failure or judgment?*

- **Build in silence**: Let the days of 'nothing happening' be sacred—they are your roots.

- **Adjust without guilt**: Changing your method is not the same as giving up. Sometimes we must replant the seed in a different soil.

- **Listen to your body and soul**: Resistance in the body is not always laziness. Sometimes, it's life saying, "Pause. Reroute."

Closing Words in the Glow of Buddha Hall

The wind outside whispered through the trees. A leaf danced down and settled gently near the steps. Guruji's voice softened, almost merging with the evening.

"True mastery is not found in relentless pushing or in passive waiting. It is found in the sacred dance between persistence and surrender—knowing when to act, when to listen, and when to simply trust the tide."

"The sea always returns the egg—not because we shouted, but because we stayed."

A deep stillness filled the hall—not empty, but full. The kind of silence that only arrives when truth has gently landed.

Fireplace Gathering – Night Whispers under a Clouded Sky

The fire cracked softly, casting flickering shadows onto the worn stones. The wind whistled through the tall grasses as if carrying the echoes of Buddha Hall into the night. Fireflies danced like wandering thoughts—silent, golden, and weightless.

The devotees had circled around the fire after a quiet dinner. A kind of sacred tiredness hung in the air—not of exhaustion, but of being deeply moved. Words were fewer now. Hearts were open.

Apeksha, sitting with her knees pulled to her chest, looked at the others. The flames reflected in her eyes.

She spoke softly.

"Let me tell you a story from one of my earlier retreats… A moment I've never quite forgotten."

The Lantern That Wouldn't Light

"It was a few years ago, during a winter retreat in the hills. The nights were longer then, and silence came faster. One evening, I was asked to light the path from the main hall to the dormitories using old clay lanterns."

"I went eagerly, holding a small bundle of wicks and a bottle of oil. Each lantern needed care. I remember the satisfaction of seeing one light up—warm and steady in the night."

"But then, I came to the last lantern. It was placed near an old mango tree. No matter how many times I tried—changing the wick, adding oil, shielding it from the wind—it would not light."

"I was growing frustrated, shivering. Others had gone to rest. I could have walked away. But something in me said, *'Stay.'* Not out of pride. But because… I felt that lantern mattered."

"I knelt beside it. I prayed. Not with words. Just presence. Stillness. I stopped trying and simply… waited."

"And then… a spark."

"Not from my matchstick—but from within the lantern itself. A faint glow. I was startled. I still don't know how it happened. But it lit itself."

The Deeper Message

Apeksha's voice trembled slightly, not with sadness, but with reverence.

"That night, I learned something that no book could've taught me: Sometimes, the light comes not through effort, but through *presence*. Not from forcing, but from surrendering into trust."

"That lantern… it was me. All the times I tried to fix, control, strive. And all the while, what it really needed was *stillness*. A silent invitation. A soft kind of faith."

Whispers Around the Fire

There was silence around the fire—not empty, but full.

Lalitha broke it first, her voice hushed.

"It really touched… especially the part where you said the light came not through effort, but through presence."

Nita nodded slowly, her palms curled around her warm tea.

"Yes… I felt like I was that lantern, waiting for something inside me to finally say yes to the light."

Vasudeva and Vidyarthi looked at each other, then at Apeksha.

"You're gifted," Vasudeva said.

"It wasn't just a story. It was a mirror." Vidyarthi added.

The Sacred Pause Before Tomorrow

Above them, the sky had hidden the stars behind thick, hurried clouds. But no one seemed to mind. The fireflies hadn't stopped dancing. The wind had not lost its song.

And in the hush between words and the lull of night, something had shifted. Perhaps it was the collective understanding that not all things need to be fixed. Some simply need to be *witnessed*.

As the fire slowly died and the group dispersed for rest, Apeksha stayed back for a moment—her hand hovering near the warmth. She didn't speak. She didn't smile.

She just sat—like that old lantern.

Lit from within.

PART THREE

Living the Attraction

Integration, Radiance, and Legacy

"When your inner world and outer actions harmonise, you radiate a magnetic light—one that not only draws abundance but leaves a legacy of inspiration for generations to come."

-Shree Shambav

CHAPTER IX
Rule 8 – Practising Gratitude

"What you appreciate expands—gratitude is the invisible force that pulls blessings closer."

– *Shree Shambav*

Synopsis

Gratitude is more than a polite gesture—it is a profound, soul-rooted force that magnetises abundance and joy into your life. This chapter unveils how deep, authentic gratitude transforms your energetic vibration and enhances the Law of Attraction. When you cultivate a grateful heart, you align with the flow of giving and receiving, opening channels for miracles.

You will explore powerful daily rituals, the practice of gratitude journaling, and ways to nurture a genuinely grateful attitude that persists beyond circumstances. Gratitude shifts your focus from lack to plenty, rewiring your subconscious to recognise and attract more of what you cherish.

A Morning in Kumbhariyur – The Story Before the Silence

The morning in **Kumbhariyur** had the hush of grace. The wind moved softly, carrying the scent of damp earth and flowering neem. The sky, a shade of pearl-grey, seemed to watch over the village with quiet wisdom.

Akshaya, wrapped in a shawl, walked alongside Vasudeva, their breath visible in the early chill. The soil beneath their feet was cool, and their steps, unhurried. In the distance, they spotted Padma, Roopa, and Akshatha huddled near the peepal grove, their laughter mingling gently with the rustling leaves.

"Hot coffee," Akshaya grinned, rubbing his palms together, "feels like the sacred call of the morning."

Padma chuckled, "A cup of warmth before wisdom. Yes, I'd say we've earned it."

Soon, others drifted in—Apeksha, serene and observant; Kiran, thoughtful as always. The group stood beneath a banyan tree, the grass underfoot kissed by dew, each blade glistening like a tiny prayer. The birds were busy with morning chores—fluttering, gathering, calling. Nature, it seemed, had already begun her day with devotion.

They stood in a semi-circle, hands warming over small earthen cups of coffee. The steam rose like whispers of incense.

Apeksha, after a sip and a silence, gently said, "Do you remember the story Guruji once shared at the last retreat? No, not one from scriptures—but the one that happened right here."

They nodded, leaning in slightly.

Apeksha's Story – *The Forgotten Lamp*

"There was a girl," Apeksha began, "her name was Meghna, and she had once come to this very village. She was young, full of dreams, but easily swayed by doubt. She carried within her a question she could not answer: *'Am I worthy of the life I desire?'*

"She had joined a retreat just like ours. Every morning, she'd walk this very path, much like we just did, wondering if something would 'click'—some sign, some miracle, to prove her worth.

"One night, during the retreat, the power went out. Total darkness. The village was asleep, but Meghna could not rest. She walked out, barefoot, and wandered toward the fields. She stumbled near the old shrine at the edge of the hill."

Apeksha paused. The group leaned closer.

"There, she found a small clay lamp, forgotten, half-buried in the soil. And somehow, without knowing why, she decided to clean it, fill it with oil from her satchel, and light it using the matchsticks she carried from her room. The flame flickered to life.

"She sat there, watching the light in the vast dark. In that moment, she didn't feel small or lost. She didn't ask if she was worthy. She didn't demand an answer. She just *was*. That light—modest, imperfect—was *enough*. She realised then: *Your light doesn't need to be seen by the world to be sacred. It just needs to be lit, consistently, courageously.*"

Apeksha looked up, her voice softer now.

"Sometimes," she whispered, "we wait for the world to confirm our radiance. But the soul already knows. We just have to remember to light the lamp—again and again."

There was silence. Not the awkward kind, but the *still* kind. The kind that lives in between heartbeats.

Lalitha wiped a tear. Roopa placed a hand on Apeksha's shoulder. Kiran looked up at the sky. The clouds had parted slightly. A single ray touched the banyan leaves.

"Time for the session," Kiran said, his voice almost reverent.

And slowly, they began walking toward **Buddha Hall**, their footsteps gentle, as if not to disturb the grace that had just visited them.

Inside the hall, mats were laid, incense curled into the air, and a bell chimed softly.

But before any words were spoken that day, they had already heard a truth—told not from a podium, but from the quiet courage of a soul who remembered to light her own forgotten lamp.

Gratitude and the Cup of Receiving

After a few minutes of sacred stillness, Guruji entered Buddha Hall, his presence gentle, yet unmistakably grounding. The faint fragrance of sandalwood lingered in the air. The devotees sat silently, their minds still absorbing the story Apeksha had told under the banyan tree.

Guruji bowed toward the lamp that flickered at the altar and then took his seat. The hall, already silent, seemed to deepen into another layer of stillness.

Then, Aastha, seated near the front with her notebook open and her eyes tender, softly asked, "Guruji, how does our current relationship with gratitude influence our ability to manifest our desires?"

Guruji looked at her, then let his gaze sweep gently across the room. He smiled with a quiet wisdom, as though Aastha had asked a question that belonged to many hearts.

The Clay Cup and the Overflow

Guruji began, "Many years ago, in the northern hills, I met a potter. He was old and bent, his hands white with clay. I asked him what made a pot strong. He said something I never forgot: *'It is not what you put into the clay that makes the pot strong, but what you remove.'*"

He paused, letting that thought settle.

"Desires are like water," he continued, "clear, flowing, vibrant. But gratitude… gratitude is the cup. Without the cup, water spills, scatters, and is lost. Without gratitude, desire cannot be held. It leaks away through complaints, comparisons, and inner scarcity."

A few heads nodded slowly.

"Let me tell you a story," he said.

The Story of the Two Farmers

"Two farmers prayed for rain.

Both had sown their seeds. Both wanted a good harvest. But one of them, every day, went to his fields, cleared weeds, removed stones, sang to his crops, and prepared a water channel in faith. The other waited indoors, grumbling, 'What's the point? The rains never comes when I need them.'

When the rains finally came, they fell equally on both lands. But only one field was ready to receive it. The other was flooded, wasted, and lost.

Desire is the rain. Gratitude is the readiness.

When we carry resentment, complaint, or entitlement, we unconsciously close the gates of receiving. The universe whispers, 'If you cannot honour what is, how will you cherish what is coming?'"

The Gentle Power of Gratitude

"Gratitude," Guruji said softly, "is not just a feeling. It is an energetic alignment. A frequency that says, *'I trust life. I honour what is. I am ready to receive more.'* Not because I lack, but because I cherish."

He leaned forward slightly, his voice lower now.

"If you feel stuck in your manifestations, don't ask first, 'What am I missing?' Ask instead, *'What have I stopped appreciating?'*

Sometimes, the gateway to everything you want is found in loving everything you already have."

A soft silence followed. The kind of silence that feels like a collective breath held in reverence.

Vidyarthi whispered, "It's so simple... yet I forget."

Guruji nodded, "That's why we practise. Gratitude is not a reaction; it is a discipline. A remembering. And in that remembrance, we shape our energy into a vessel strong enough to hold miracles."

A bell chimed. A wind stirred the edges of the saffron drapes.

The day had begun—not with effort, but with grace.

The faint scent of incense still lingered. A single ray of morning sun filtered through the open window, falling on the edge of Guruji's seat. Outside, a koel called through the stillness. Within, the space felt sacred, woven with silence and sincerity.

Vasudeva, always composed and inward-looking. With reverence in his voice, he asked, "Guruji, what daily rituals or practices help us connect to a deeper, more consistent sense of gratitude?"

Guruji didn't speak right away. Instead, he closed his eyes, and in that pause, time itself seemed to take a breath.

Then he began, his voice quiet, warm like the first light of dawn:

The Ritual of the Lamp and the Offering of the Day

"Years ago," Guruji said, "in a small village I visited during monsoon, there lived an old woman named

Janaki Amma. Every morning before sunrise, she would step out, even in the rain, and light a small earthen lamp under the ancient peepal tree near her hut."

"She would offer just three grains of rice and a flower. Every day. No matter how poor, how tired, how stormy the skies were—she lit that lamp and made that offering. And then she would say, *Thank you, life, for one more dawn to serve.*"

"One day I asked her, *Why, Amma? You have so little. What is this ritual for?* She smiled and replied, *If I wait for something big to happen before I feel thankful, I'll miss the thousands of tiny miracles happening now. My breath is a miracle. This lamp is a miracle. Gratitude is how I stay rich even when I have nothing.*"

Gratitude is a Muscle, Not a Mood

"Gratitude," Guruji said, turning gently toward Vasudeva, "is like a well. If you don't draw from it daily, the water goes stale or sinks too deep to reach. But with small, consistent rituals, we keep the waters clear."

"Here are a few rituals I invite you to explore—not as obligations, but as sacred doorways into daily thankfulness."

1. The Morning Touch

"Before your feet touch the ground upon waking, place your hand on your heart. Whisper, *'Thank you, life, for returning me to this day.'* No phone. No to-do list. Just a moment to acknowledge existence."

2. The Gratitude Pebble

"Carry a small stone in your pocket. Let it be your silent reminder. Each time your hand brushes it, pause and name one thing you are grateful for at that exact moment. It grounds your awareness into presence."

3. The Evening Candle

"Light a candle at sunset. Sit in silence for three minutes. Recall one challenge of the day and offer gratitude for its hidden teaching. Gratitude is not only for comfort—it is the **alchemy of discomfort** into wisdom."

4. The Thankfulness Journal

"Write down three things you appreciated that day—but here's the key: make them different each day. This trains your mind to search for beauty in overlooked corners: a stranger's smile, a cool breeze, a kind word you offered."

5. Service as Gratitude in Motion

"Do one small act of kindness anonymously. Help someone, feed a bird, sweep a space—not to be seen, but to feel connected. Gratitude is most alive when it flows outward."

Guruji turned toward the assembly now, his voice deep with compassion.

"Gratitude is not a reaction—it is a **state of relationship with life.** The more we practice it, the more we begin to see that everything—yes, even pain—has something to give."

"Don't wait for joy to be grateful. Be grateful, and you'll find joy has quietly walked in."

A hush fell over the hall. Some devotees closed their eyes, others wiped tears that had silently traced their cheeks.

The breeze that flowed in from the stone windows carried the scent of earth and marigold. Devotees had gathered in a still hall, their hearts open after a long day of introspection. Padma, her voice soft but clear, asked:

"Guruji, how might keeping a gratitude journal change the way we perceive our life and our manifestations over time?"

Guruji looked at her with the gentleness who had tasted many seasons of change. He closed his eyes for a moment, as if scanning the memory of a lifetime, and began.

The Farmer's Ledger of Light

"There was once a humble farmer named Aran who lived in the hills of Wayanad. He had a small patch of land, not fertile by most standards, but he treated it with deep devotion. Every evening after working the fields, instead of counting only what he lacked—rainfall, yield, better tools—he would sit by his lamp and write in what he called his *'Ledger of Light.'*"

"In this tattered journal, he recorded not the struggles of the day, but the **small miracles**—the bees that had returned to the guava tree, the smile of his child, a neighbour's unexpected help, the softness of the rain on his skin."

"For years, he wrote—not grand things, just *truthful little moments*. At first, it seemed like nothing. But something subtle began to change."

The Shift in Seeing

"Over time, Aran's *eyes became seasoned with beauty*. He began to **notice** what others rushed past. His field hadn't changed. His income hadn't multiplied. But *his heart had grown full*, alert to the grace within each breath."

"One day, a neighbour asked him, 'How do you remain so content with so little?' Aran smiled and said, 'Because I count what is present, not what is absent. And the more I count it, the more it grows.'"

Gratitude Journaling: A Sacred Mirror

Guruji turned to Padma and the devotees.

"Keeping a gratitude journal is not about pretending everything is perfect. It is about **training your mind to see what the soul already knows**—that life, even in its simplest form, is an unfolding miracle."

"When you write your gratitude—daily, honestly, quietly—you are building a new set of eyes. Eyes that see not only what's happening but what's *blessing you silently*. Over time, you begin to manifest differently—not from hunger, but from fullness. You are no longer chasing something to complete you. You are co-creating from a place that already feels whole."

The Law of Subtle Expansion

"You see," Guruji continued, "what you appreciate… appreciates. The moment you bless something with attention, it begins to bloom under your gaze. This is not magic—it's energetic mathematics."

"Gratitude is the **magnetism of the soul**. The more you record it, the more you reinforce a neural path of abundance. And over time, this path becomes the highway through which your manifestations travel."

The Journal Becomes a Temple

"That simple notebook," he whispered, "becomes a sacred space. A temple of memory, resilience, and reverence. When storms hit—and they will—you will open its pages, and there, like stars in the night, your own past awakenings will remind you of the light."

Padma lowered her eyes, tears glimmering—not from sorrow, but from a soul that had just remembered something it always knew.

All around her, devotees sat in silence. Some made a note to begin their journal that night.

And somewhere inside, something shifted.

CHAPTER X

Rule 9 – Surrounding Yourself with Positive Influences

"The energy you surround yourself with either fuels your dreams or dims your light."

– Shree Shambav

Synopsis

Your environment profoundly shapes your energy and, by extension, your ability to manifest. This chapter uncovers the importance of cultivating emotional detox and creating energetic spaces that uplift and inspire you. Surrounding yourself with positive influences—from people to media—acts like fertile soil, nurturing your dreams and accelerating your growth.

You'll learn how to consciously build a supportive social circle, cleanse your physical and emotional surroundings from negativity, and curate the content you consume. Aligning your external environment with your inner intentions creates a powerful synergy that strengthens your manifestation journey.

Akshaya leaned forward gently and asked, "Guruji, how do the people we spend the most time with influence our mindset, energy, and belief in our manifestations?"

Guruji, seated with a still presence, let the question breathe into the silence. Then, with a calm gaze that saw far deeper than the surface, he began.

The Forest of Becoming

"Akshaya," he said softly, "imagine you are a sapling—a young tree planted in a vast forest. Around you, there are other trees: some tall and proud, reaching for the sun; others twisted, gnarled from storms; some leaning close, offering shade; others competing for light. You do not grow in isolation. Every tree around you—through their shade or light, their roots or fragrance—**influences your becoming**."

"The people we spend time with are like these trees in our forest of life. Their beliefs, their words, their silences, their habits—whether encouraging or fearful—create an emotional ecosystem in which we either flourish or wither."

The Candle Room Story

"Let me share a story," Guruji continued, his voice a steady stream under the darkening sky.

"There was a young woman named Diya, full of light, dreams, and a yearning to bring something meaningful into the world. She lived in a town where most people had forgotten their own light. They would mock her enthusiasm, dismiss her ideas, and warn her constantly—*'Be realistic. Don't dream so much.'* Over time, Diya began to doubt herself. Her spark dimmed—not because her dream was wrong, but because her environment became a room without flame."

"One day, she visited her grandmother in the hills—a woman known for her quiet strength. That evening, as night fell, her grandmother took her into a small room filled with candles. Each one was lit. The room shimmered."

"She said, 'This is what it feels like when you surround yourself with people who believe in light. They don't just see you—they remind you of yourself when you forget. They hold the mirror when your vision blurs.'"

"'And when you surround yourself with cynics and doubters, it's like walking with a wet cloth around your flame. Eventually, the fire suffocates.'"

The Vibration of Influence

Guruji looked around the hall. "We are energy beings. We tune ourselves daily—consciously or unconsciously—to the **frequency of those closest to**

us. If we walk with people who constantly live in scarcity, fear, or ridicule, we begin to internalise their worldview. Our manifestations slow—not because the universe isn't listening, but because we start whispering instead of declaring. We shrink."

"But when we walk with the bold-hearted, the kind, the believers, the silent seers—our energy begins to hum in alignment again. We dare. We try. We trust. We remember."

Choose Your Circle as You Would Choose Your Soil

"Your circle is your soil," Guruji said. "Would you plant a sacred seed in poisoned earth? Then why plant your dreams among voices that mock their possibility?"

"Spend time with those whose eyes light up when you speak of vision. Who challenges your fears—not your dreams. Who waters your worth when you forget how to?"

The Choice of Resonance

"As you journey into manifestation," he concluded, "ask yourself: *Who is close enough to whisper into my soul? And what are they whispering?*"

The Law of Attraction

"Your environment is not just physical—it's energetic. Protect it. Curate it. Walk with those who remind you of your vastness."

Akshaya sat quietly. The words sank like roots.

Around him, the others in Buddha Hall sat in silence—not the silence of absence, but of deep inner listening. A few closed their eyes. A few opened their journals. Something had shifted.

Not loudly.

But deeply.

The Buddha Hall was soaked in stillness. The air smelled of vetiver and sandalwood. Around Guruji, the disciples sat in patient reflection, hearts open after a long morning of sacred silence.

Then, softly, Roopa spoke.

"Guruji, what areas of your physical or emotional environment feel cluttered or draining, and how might you begin a detox process?"

Guruji didn't answer immediately. He closed his eyes. Then he opened them and began.

The Old Courtyard and the Choked Well

"There was once an old courtyard in a monastery far away," he said, his voice low and rhythmic, "and at the centre of this courtyard was a well. It was ancient. It had served generations—offering clear, sweet water. But over the years, leaves had fallen into it. Dust gathered. A broken broom was left leaning against its rim. Slowly, the water darkened. Fewer monks came to draw from it."

"One day, a novice monk noticed this and asked the abbot, *'Has the well gone dry?'*"

"The abbot smiled and said, *'No, child. It's just hidden beneath what it was never meant to hold.'*"

"So they began the work. Gently, they removed the leaves. They swept the courtyard. They lowered a lamp into the well to check its depth. It took days. But one morning, as the first light kissed the stone, they saw the bottom again. The water was still there. Clear. Waiting."

Our Inner Courtyard

"Roopa," Guruji continued, turning to her with warmth, "we all have such a courtyard inside us—our environment, our emotional space. And like that well, we begin our lives full of clarity and aliveness. But slowly, without noticing, small things gather—resentments, half-finished conversations, objects we no longer love, roles we no longer fit, and energies that don't belong to us."

"They collect like fallen leaves—harmless at first, but eventually, they veil our clarity, cloud our peace, and dull our sensitivity to the soul's whisper."

Clutter Isn't Just Stuff—It's Unspoken Emotion

"Detox is not just cleaning our rooms," Guruji said, "it is **making room**—for life, for breath, for truth."

"Ask yourself: What are the objects in my space that carry memories I've outgrown? Which relationships leave me tired, not nourished? What are the thoughts that loop in my mind like restless birds that never land?"

"These are your leaves in the well."

The Gentle Burn

"Detox," he said, "is not a harsh cleansing. It's a *compassionate release*. Like gently burning dried leaves to make space for new soil. You don't attack the clutter—you bless it. You thank it for what it once meant. And then, you let it go."

A Personal Story – The Shelf of Shadows

Guruji looked around the hall, his voice more intimate now.

"There was once a small wooden shelf in my old cottage—a shelf I hadn't touched for years. It had letters, trinkets, and photos. One rainy evening, I sat before it. I didn't know why. But something in me whispered, *'It's time.'*"

"I opened each letter. Some made me smile. Others, weep. Some brought bitterness. I realised: I had been carrying old identities, stories that no longer reflected who I had become. That night, I lit a small flame and let go—one letter at a time. Not in anger, but in honour."

"When I woke up the next morning, something had changed. Not outside. But inside. I felt…light. Empty in the most peaceful way. That shelf now holds only three things: a small lamp, a white feather, and a poem. The rest, I carry in memory, not weight."

Letting the Soul Breathe Again

"So, Roopa," Guruji said, voice soft as wind, "detox begins when we no longer fear emptiness. When we trust that letting go is not loss—it is **liberation**."

"Make space. Sweep the well. Bless what was. And watch how silence begins to sing again. Your manifestations… your peace… your creativity… they are not lost. They are waiting beneath the leaves."

The Buddha Hall sat in reverent stillness. No one spoke. But something invisible was shifting—like inner windows being opened one by one. Roopa smiled gently, her eyes glassy with emotion.

The detox had already begun.

Vasudeva, gently raised his voice into the silence: "Guruji, how does the media and content we regularly consume affect our thoughts, feelings, and vibration?"

Guruji leaned slightly forward. A moment passed before he spoke.

The Well and the Spoon of Salt

"Imagine," Guruji began, "you have a crystal-clear bowl of water before you. Into this bowl, each morning, you drop a spoon of salt. Just one spoon. It's small. You don't think it matters."

"But as the days pass, the water becomes heavier, clouded. The flavour changes. The transparency dims. And eventually, what was once pure now tastes unpleasant."

He paused. "Now replace that water with your *mind*, your *heart*, your *inner field of vibration*. And the salt? The content you consume—every article, every news headline, every dramatic video, every mindless scroll. What seems harmless in isolation becomes, over time, a slow poisoning of your frequency."

The Whisper Behind the Words

"Media," Guruji said softly, "does not merely *inform*. It *imprints*."

"It's not just about what we read or hear—it's about what those messages *tell us to feel*. That we're not enough. That danger is constant. That speed is superior to stillness. That comparison is natural. That outrage is the truth."

"And so, quietly, without realising it, your thoughts become agitated, your emotional body contracts, and your manifestations slow—not because life has changed, but because your inner receiver is tuned to static, not signal."

A Story from a Village School

"I once visited a small school in a village that had no internet. No television. Just books, stories, and long walks under the sky. I sat with a group of children who spoke like poets. Their metaphors were rich. Their questions were deep. One little girl said to me, 'The moon never complains about the sun's brightness. She just waits for her turn to shine.'"

Guruji smiled. "She was nine."

He looked around the hall. "I realised that without the noise of media telling them *how* to think, they were *still thinking*, but freely. Feeling deeply. Imagining fully."

Your Vibration is Sacred Soil

"You see," Guruji said, "manifestation doesn't come from your mind alone. It comes from the *vibration* of your entire being. And that vibration is like soil. If you pour oil, plastic, and acid into it every day—even in drops—it stops growing what you desire."

"But when you feed it sunlight, silence, poetry, nature, honest conversation, and beauty—it becomes a field of miracles."

A Practical Reminder

"So, Vasudeva," Guruji continued gently, "if you find your thoughts racing, your heart closed, your fears louder than your dreams—ask not only *what am I thinking?* but *what have I been absorbing?*"

"Would you eat food someone stirred with a dirty spoon? No. But many feed their minds from unfiltered hands every hour."

The Clean Diet of the Soul

"Begin a soul diet," he whispered. "One day a week, go without news. Replace scrolling with sacred reading. Watch something that makes you cry with reverence. Play music that melts your fear. Sit in nature without taking a photo."

"These small changes are not luxury. They are *alchemy*."

"Because whatever you let in," Guruji concluded, "will begin to speak through you—your words, your choices, your dreams. Choose what deserves that power."

Silence fell like snowfall. Even the trees outside seemed to be still.

Vasudeva bowed his head, visibly moved. Around the Buddha Hall, eyes closed in quiet contemplation— some in tears, some with a new resolve.

The air hummed with one collective realisation:

We are always manifesting.

But what we consume… decides what we manifest.

Apeksha, her voice filled with warmth and wonder, asked: "Guruji, what qualities do we seek in our tribe—our community—that support and amplify our vision?"

The Garden That Blooms Together

"Imagine your soul as a seed," Guruji began. "Your dreams, your purpose, your visions—they are the inner tree waiting to grow. But no seed blossoms in isolation. It needs *climate*, *soil*, *sunlight*, and *companionship*. It needs a *garden*."

"In the garden of manifestation, your *tribe* is the environment around your roots. It determines whether your dreams are nourished… or neglected."

The Story of the Silent Shell

"I once visited a coastal village," Guruji continued. "There was a young boy who had found a rare, spiralled shell. Beautiful. But the elders warned him, 'It will lose its colour if it's kept alone on the shelf.'"

"He didn't understand, but he placed it high up anyway. Years passed. The shell dulled. One day, the boy—now grown—went diving and found more of the same shells on the ocean floor. But he noticed something curious."

"They were vibrant. Alive in colour. Resonant in sound when you held them to your ear. Why? Because they were **together**—in saltwater, in movement, in *community*. They held each other's lives."

Your Tribe Is the Mirror and the Wind

Guruji turned to the devotees.

"A good community does not just support your dream—it *reminds you of it* when you forget. It reflects the light in you when your own clouds blind you. It celebrates your steps without competition. It challenges you to rise without crushing your spirit."

"They are the mirror that shows you your soul's true face, and the wind that gently pushes your boat when your arms are tired."

The Moon Circle

"In the Himalayas," Guruji said, "I met a group of seekers who would sit in silence every full moon. No talking. Just presence. They believed that **when hearts align without words, visions rise like tides**."

"I asked them why they gathered even when life got busy. One woman said, 'Because we remember differently when we remember together.'"

What to Seek in Your Tribe

He raised his hand and gently pointed his fingers in rhythm as he listed:

- "Seek those who **listen to your silence**, not just your words.

- Seek those who are **rooted in their own journey**, yet rejoice in yours.

- Seek those who can sit with your **doubt without feeding it**, but also speak with fire when your flame dims.

- Seek those who ask, *'How can I serve your vision?'* instead of *'How does it serve me?'*

- And above all," Guruji said, voice low and glowing, "seek those who will **pray with you**, not just cheer for you."

A Personal Reflection

He looked at Apeksha and said gently, "There were times in my path when I was surrounded by people who loved me, but did not understand my journey. They gave advice, but not insight. They offered comfort, but not clarity. It felt lonely in a crowd."

"But when I found those whose hearts pulsed with similar longing—not the same answers, but the same questions—I felt seen without needing to explain.

And from that moment, my manifestations flowed not faster, but *truer*."

"So," Guruji whispered, "don't just seek a tribe that claps when you shine. Find those who sit with you in the mud, who help you tend the roots, who water your soul *before* the fruit appears. Because when your tribe is right, your vision becomes not a burden, but a shared song."

The hall remained still. Apeksha smiled, her eyes moist. Around her, heads nodded not just in agreement, but in *recognition*—each heart recalling those rare souls who had stood by them like unseen pillars.

The bells chimed softly outside.

And in that moment, every soul in Buddha Hall knew:

A true tribe is not made of many.

It's made of the few…

…who see the divine in you even when you forget it yourself.

The morning mist in Kumbhariyur hadn't lifted yet. It curled between the blades of dew-kissed grass and wove through the slender trunks of sandalwood trees like an ancient whisper. Birds stirred gently, not yet in full song, as though even nature chose silence over noise.

Guruji had just concluded the early discourse and invited everyone to take a short **morning break**.

Beneath the wide, old Banyan tree, Abhilasha, Akanksh, Akshatha, Apeksha, and Roopa gathered quietly, each holding the stillness of the session like a sacred thread in their palms. The air was infused with the grounding aroma of sandalwood, the earthiness of vetiver, and the faint bitterness of brewing coffee from the Ashram kitchen nearby.

Kiran, Sam, Alice, Sofia, Bhavya, Aarna, Dev, and John took a slow stroll through the garden path, whispering reflections or simply walking in silence—hearts full, minds light.

Nita and Lalitha, ever thoughtful, appeared soon after—carrying a tray of clay cups filled with steaming coffee and fragrant tulsi tea. They handed them out with quiet smiles, the clink of pottery against pottery forming a rhythm of humble offering.

The Story That Stilled the Morning

As the warmth of coffee thawed their fingers, Apeksha gently placed her cup down on the root of the banyan tree and said, "Many years ago, when I first came to Kumbhariyur... something happened I've never forgotten."

The group leaned in, not from curiosity, but reverence.

The Story of the Wounded Deer

"There was a young deer," Apeksha began, her eyes distant, "that had strayed into the outer edge of the Ashram Forest one summer evening. I was walking near the lotus pond when I heard rustling—then a thud. It had been caught in a hunter's trap, likely left by someone from a nearby village."

"I remember kneeling beside it. Its leg was bleeding, eyes wide with pain—but there was no fight in it. Only a trembling stillness, as if its spirit had half-left the body."

"I didn't know what to do. I was new to these woods. But something in me didn't panic. I just... sat beside it. I sang. I cried. I whispered that it would live."

"Eventually, the Ashram caretakers arrived. They freed it and carried it to the shelter. That deer... it survived. But something else survived too: a realisation."

Apeksha paused. Her fingers traced a fallen banyan leaf.

"Your Presence is a Healing Field"

She continued, "That day, I understood something. You don't always need answers, medicines, or solutions. Sometimes, *you just need to stay*. To witness. To love. To hold pain like a fragile ember until the fire of life remembers itself."

"That moment changed me. And since then, I've tried to be that space—not for deer, but for people. For myself. For the broken parts within me."

The Silence that Followed

No one spoke for a long time.

The wind rustled gently through the leaves above, almost like an unseen hand had reached out to bless Apeksha's heart. The coffee in their cups had cooled, but no one minded. Something warmer was flowing through them now.

Kieron finally whispered, "Apeksha, your story... was touching."
Everyone nodded silently.

Vasudeva, ever stoic, looked up at the tree and murmured, "It wasn't a story. It was a mirror."

Kiran looked at his watch and sighed, "It's time for the session."
But even he didn't move for a while.

The group lingered—not out of reluctance, but reverence.
They knew the next session had already begun. It just wasn't in Buddha Hall.

It had begun **right there**, under the old Banyan, in the quiet remembering of what it means to be present—*fully, lovingly, and humanly.*

Message and Insight:

Sometimes, the sacred work isn't in doing or fixing—it is in staying.

In a world rushing to resolve, the one who can stay with pain, patiently and lovingly, becomes the true healer.

Your tribe doesn't just need your strength—they need your presence.

CHAPTER XI

Rule 10 – Embracing Change

"When you stop fighting change, you allow life's river to carry you to new and wondrous shores."

– Shree Shambav

Synopsis

Change is the gateway to growth, yet it often stirs fear and resistance within us. This chapter invites you to transmute fear into flow by welcoming change as an essential part of your manifestation journey. Instead of clinging to comfort and certainty, you'll learn to embrace adaptability, seeing change not as a threat but as a powerful catalyst for unexpected blessings.

By cultivating flexibility and learning to navigate uncertainty with grace, you open yourself to new opportunities and expanded possibilities. Change becomes a positive force, shaping your path and deepening your resilience, creativity, and self-trust.

Akanksh, though calm, held a quiet intensity.

"Guruji," he began, "How do we typically respond to change—do we resist, fear, or embrace it—and what stories or beliefs influence this response?"

Guruji slowly opened his eyes, his gaze settling like still water on Akanksh. A moment of silence passed, not empty, but pregnant with listening.

He finally spoke, voice low and rich like rain over earth:

"The Tree That Refused to Bend"

"Akanksh," Guruji said, "let me tell you a story—from a life I once witnessed closely."

"There was once a grand peepul tree that stood tall in the centre of a village I visited during my early years. Towering, proud, rooted deep—it was a symbol of strength. The villagers often gathered beneath it for shade, stories, and silence. But the tree had a secret: it feared change.

One year, strong winds began to frequent the region. Seasons grew unpredictable. Every tree around the peepul began to sway, shed leaves early, or bend gently with the wind. But not this one. It resisted. It stiffened. It stood unmoved—trying to be the unshakable pillar it had always been.

Then came the storm.

A storm so fierce that the earth itself seemed to tremble. Trees that had bent low—bending like dancers in surrender—survived. But the peepul, in its refusal to yield, cracked at the trunk. It fell. Its roots, though deep, had grown rigid, refusing the nourishment of movement."

Guruji paused. The hall was quiet, each listener absorbed.

The Inner Roots of Resistance

He continued, "We often do the same, Akanksh. Our minds tell us that change means loss. Our conditioning whispers: *safety lies in the known*. And so, we build walls around routines, identities, and beliefs.

But what we forget is this: change is not the enemy—it is the sculptor. It doesn't arrive to destroy, but to chisel away what is no longer needed. Our resistance isn't to change itself; it's to the story we've attached to what change means—stories inherited from fear, from culture, from wounds unhealed.

Some believe change means they've failed. Others fear that embracing change will erase who they are. But the truth is—change reveals who you are beneath the roles you cling to."

The River's Way

"Let me offer you another image," Guruji said gently. "The river does not resist the rock in its path. It doesn't complain, nor does it fear. It curves. It carves. It adapts.

That is not weakness. That is intelligence guided by trust."

He turned to the hall.

"To resist change is to grip an identity that may no longer serve your growth. To fear it is human. But to stay frozen is to refuse your own evolution. Embrace it like the river. Flow through it. And you'll find that what feels like an end… is often a re-beginning dressed in unfamiliar clothes."

"Akanksh," Guruji concluded, "Ask yourself—not just how you respond to change—but **who taught you to fear it?** Was it a wound? A heartbreak? A voice from your childhood?

When you become aware of the source of your story, you no longer have to live by it. You can write a new one."

The Buddha Hall remained still.

A single tear escaped from Apeksha's cheek. Abhirami gently reached out and held her hand. Kiran closed his eyes.

Abhilasha, softly raised her voice after a moment of silence.

"Guruji," she asked with honest eyes, "In what ways can embracing uncertainty create space for new opportunities and personal growth in our lives?"

Guruji looked toward her, with a faint smile.

The Dance of the Unknown

"Abhilasha," he began, "life is not a straight road—it is a winding river, and that river doesn't ask the mountains to move. It flows. Sometimes fast, sometimes still. And always uncertain."

He paused, then said: "Let me tell you a story."

The Fisherman and the Fog

"There once lived an old fisherman named Raman in a coastal village of Mangalur. Every morning, he would set sail before dawn, casting his net at a spot his father had passed down to him. It was known to bring an abundant catch.

One morning, a dense fog fell over the sea. Raman couldn't find the familiar landmarks. He panicked—rowing aimlessly, afraid he would return empty-handed or lose his way entirely.

But after some time, he noticed something strange—the feel of the water had changed. It was cooler, deeper. He cast his net hesitantly... and when he pulled it back, it was full—richer than any haul he'd ever known.

He had, without realising it, drifted into new waters. Uncertainty had taken him where intention never dared to go.

From that day on, Raman no longer feared the fog. He welcomed it. He called it his teacher."

Embracing the Unknown

Guruji looked across the hall. "You see, Abhilasha, we often treat uncertainty as a threat, but it is in fact an **invitation**—to go beyond habit, beyond plans, beyond the limited identity we've outgrown."

"We try to control outcomes, fearing what we cannot predict. But true growth doesn't occur within the known—it occurs in the trembling space of not knowing, in the surrender to the unfolding. When you embrace uncertainty, you create **space**—and space is where grace enters."

He pointed gently to his heart.

"Certainty is of the mind. Expansion is of the soul. And the soul thrives not by knowing, but by trusting."

The Caterpillar's Surrender

"Think of the caterpillar," Guruji continued. "It wraps itself in darkness, dissolves into a formless mush within the cocoon. It does not know what it will become. That is uncertainty in its purest form. But because it surrenders, something extraordinary emerges."

He looked toward Abhilasha with warmth.

"So the next time life grows unclear, do not grip the steering wheel tighter. Instead, soften. Listen. Let go of who you were, so you can meet who you are becoming."

"Uncertainty," Guruji said finally, "is the womb of creation. Only when you step into the unknown can something truly new be born—from within you, around you, and through you."

The hall was silent, but not still. A quiet stirring moved within each devotee—an inner trembling, a call to surrender control and walk, even if slowly, toward the fog of the unknown.

And just then, a soft breeze entered the Buddha Hall, lifting the curtain ever so slightly, as if even nature wished to whisper:

"Step forward. You are held."

Akshaya raised his voice with calm clarity.

"Guruji," he asked, "what practices or mindsets help us cultivate adaptability and flexibility during times of transition?"

Guruji slowly opened his eyes, as though returning from a quiet inner journey. Then, with a soft gaze, he said—

The Tree That Bends

"Akshaya," Guruji began, "have you ever stood under a coconut tree during a monsoon storm?"

Akshaya smiled faintly and nodded.

"Notice how it bends?" Guruji continued. "It bends with the wind. It does not resist the storm. It does not try to out-muscle nature. Instead, it surrenders—not out of weakness, but out of wisdom."

He looked slowly around the hall.

"Resilience," he said, **"is not about being rigid. It is about knowing when to bend and when to root."**

The Weaver's Daughter

"Let me share a story," Guruji said. "Many years ago, when I was walking through a village near the Western Ghats, I stayed for a week with a family of weavers. The youngest daughter, barely fifteen, was learning the family craft from her grandmother. One evening, a fierce rain flooded their home. Their entire stock of woven cloth was destroyed."

He paused. "I assumed the girl would be devastated. But the next morning, I saw her outside, sitting cross-legged in the slush, gathering lotus stems. Curious, I asked her what she was doing."

"She smiled and said, *'Thatha(Grandfather), we can't weave today. But we can learn something new. I've heard the lotus thread is strong. Maybe the storm came to teach us that.'*"

Guruji's voice softened.

"That is adaptability—not in theory, but in the very rhythm of life. She did not wait for perfect conditions. She met life as it was—wet, uncertain, yet full of hidden threads."

Practices for the Soul in Transition

"Akshaya," Guruji said, "transitions are sacred thresholds. To walk them well, we need both strength and softness. And for that, here are a few soul-practices."

1. **Daily Inner Check-In**

"Ask yourself each morning—not 'what do I need to control today?' but 'what am I invited to release today?' Let your flexibility begin not in action, but in awareness."

2. **Journaling the Unexpected**

"Write down moments that didn't go as planned—but instead of resisting them, reflect on what they taught you. The more you see change as a guide, the less frightening it becomes."

3. **Move Like Water**

"Literally—engage in fluid movement. Tai Chi, dance, or even walking barefoot. Let the body teach the mind what it means to flow."

4. **Gratitude for the Unwritten**

"Thank the parts of your day that surprised you. Even the rough ones. This rewires your nervous system to trust change, rather than fear it."

The Inner Clay

"Akshaya," Guruji concluded, "you are like wet clay on the potter's wheel. Life will spin you—fast and dizzying at times. But if you stay moist with presence and patience, you won't crack. The hands of the Divine are shaping you. Your only task… is not to harden."

He folded his palms and looked around the hall, "Flexibility is not the opposite of strength. It *is* a strength—just wearing the clothes of surrender."

A Moment of Stillness

The hall fell silent. A single bird cooed somewhere outside. Akshaya looked down, as if absorbing something older than words. Kiran whispered to Roopa, "That… that felt like a message from the wind itself."

And in that silence, something in everyone softened—a stiff edge loosened. They could feel it. The transitions in their own lives didn't seem like punishments anymore… but invitations.

To bend. To trust. To begin again.

Roopa, leaned forward gently. Her eyes were tender but curious.

"Guruji," she asked, "Can we recall a past change that initially felt uncomfortable but later revealed itself as a blessing? What lessons did it teach us?"

The Fire at Kanakapura – A Devotee's Turning Point

The hall had quieted after Roopa's heartfelt question. Guruji gently turned his mala beads once, twice, then looked up, his eyes reflecting something tender, distant.

"Roopa," he began softly, "your question reminds me of a seeker who once came to see me... many years ago, near Kanakapura."

His voice lowered, filled with remembrance.

"He was not new to the path. He had renounced much—his career, his possessions, even his family ties, seeking peace in the forests of southern India. He had built a simple hut under an old tamarind tree. There, in solitude, he practised austerity, prayer, and long hours of meditation."

Guruji paused, as if allowing the weight of the story to settle.

"Then one monsoon night, a fierce lightning strike hit the tamarind tree behind his hut. A fire broke out. In a matter of moments, everything he had built—his journals, his wooden altar, even the hand-carved idol of Krishna—was consumed by the flames. He stood in the rain, soaked, watching it all burn… and wept."

The Shattering and the Wandering

"He told me later," Guruji continued, "that in that moment, it felt like the universe had betrayed him. He had offered everything—and yet, even the little he had left was taken. He wandered the forest aimlessly for days. Silent. Empty. Angry."

"One morning, he stumbled upon a small riverside village. An old woman, a potter, saw his torn robes and weary face. Without a word, she brought him warm food. Then, she led him to her small clay shed and asked, *Will you help me turn the wheel today?*"

The Wheel of Clay

"He stayed with her for a while. Days turned into weeks. As he worked with her, shaping mud into bowls and vessels, he began to understand something deeper. The clay needed pressure to take form. The wheel needed a steady rhythm. And sometimes, a pot collapsed—only to be reshaped again, with greater care."

Guruji smiled gently.

"The old potter once told him, 'Sometimes life takes away what we cling to—not to punish us, but to make our hands free… so we may shape something new. Something truer.'"

The Blessing in the Ashes

"That fire," Guruji said, "which he had cursed that night under the tamarind tree, eventually became his liberation. It burned not only his possessions, but his attachments. His identity as a seeker transformed into one who simply *was*. He no longer needed sacred objects to feel devotion—he became devotion. He no longer needed silence to be spiritual—he became the silence."

The Soil of Change

He looked toward Roopa and the others.

"Change rarely arrives wrapped in comfort," Guruji said. "It often comes like fire—unexpected, painful, and stripping us bare. But when we stop resisting, we find that what felt like destruction was actually preparation. Like the earth breaking open to let a seed rise."

"That seeker… he left the forest years later, not with answers—but with peace. And he told me something I never forgot: 'When everything I thought I needed was gone, I finally met myself.'"

Stillness in Buddha Hall

There was silence in the hall, deep and wide.

Roopa closed her eyes, allowing the story to settle into her bones. Aastha wiped a silent tear. Akshaya sat unmoving, a hand over his chest. Kiran whispered, "That fire lives in each of us, doesn't it?"

Guruji simply nodded.

And in that stillness, the devotees understood— *sometimes the greatest grace enters disguised as loss, but leaves behind the gift of who we were always meant to become.*

CHAPTER XII

Rule 11 – Consistent Practice and Dedication

"Consistency transforms intention into reality; devotion turns practice into a sacred dance with the universe."

– Shree Shambav

Synopsis

Manifestation is not a one-time event but a continuous journey requiring dedication and consistent practice. This chapter emphasises turning daily practices into acts of devotion—rituals that align your energy and focus with your deepest intentions. Through discipline and flow-state living, you build momentum that compounds over time, bringing your goals steadily closer.

You'll learn how to create a personalised manifestation routine, track your progress with mindful awareness, and celebrate even the smallest victories. The compound effect of persistent effort transforms fleeting motivation into lasting transformation, reinforcing your belief and connection to the Law of Attraction.

After a prolonged, sacred silence, **Greta** raised her hand gently, her voice calm but thoughtful.

"**Guruji**," she asked, "*What daily habits currently support our manifestation goals, and where could more consistency enhance our progress?*"

Guruji leaned slightly forward. "Greta," he said softly, "have you ever seen how a river shapes the stone?"

Greta nodded.

"It does not chisel it down with force in a single day. It does not hammer at it, nor does it ask the stone to change. It simply flows—daily, gently, persistently. And in time, the stone is smoothed, reshaped, transformed. *That* is the power of sacred consistency."

He paused and looked around at the others in Buddha Hall. "Most people misunderstand manifestation," he continued. "They think it is about effort in bursts—a few days of excitement, followed by restlessness or doubt. But manifestation is not an event. It is a rhythm. It is the frequency you return to when the world distracts you."

The Story of the Candle Maker

"In a small village near the Ganges," Guruji began, "there lived an old candle maker. Every morning before sunrise, he would gather wax and prepare his moulds. No matter the weather, no matter his mood, he sat at his wooden table and shaped candles—by hand, with care.

A traveller once asked him, 'Why make candles when there's no guarantee someone will buy them today?'

The candle maker replied, 'Because I don't make candles for who *might* come—I make them so that when they *do*, the light is ready.'

Many years later, his little shop became a place of pilgrimage. Not because his candles were extraordinary—but because his *devotion* was.

So too with your dreams," Guruji said, his eyes resting on Greta. "You do not practice visualisation, gratitude, or aligned action just because a result is expected tomorrow. You do them because you are preparing light. Your habits are candles lit in advance for the future you are walking into."

The Invisible Threads

"Every small, repeated action," he added, "whether it's writing your intention, keeping your mind clean, choosing faith over fear, or simply making your bed with presence—each of these habits sends out an invisible thread. And one day, you will see that they have woven a tapestry called destiny."

He looked at the room.

"But ask yourself, what are the threads you weave every day? Do you start your mornings in anxiety, scrolling through noise? Or in silence, aligning with your purpose? Do you nourish your mind with comparison—or with clarity?"

Final Teaching

"Greta," he concluded, "*consistency is not doing everything perfectly—it is doing the right things patiently, until they become who you are.* Manifestation is not summoned through intensity, but sustained through intimacy—your quiet, daily devotion to the vision life has placed in your heart."

There was a hush in the room. Greta bowed slightly, her eyes moist, her heart steadied. Others too had fallen into deep reflection, silently evaluating their mornings, their rituals, their choices.

Outside, a bird sang from the mango tree.

And somewhere deep within each listener, a candle was lit.

The Law of Attraction

Akshaya asked, "Guruji, How can we transform our manifestation practices into meaningful rituals that inspire devotion rather than obligation?"

"The difference between obligation and devotion," Guruji began softly, "is not in the action, but in the heart that offers it."

He continued, "There was a time when a young sculptor named Rivan lived in a quiet village nestled among mango groves and rivers. Every morning, he would rise early, light a lamp, and offer water to a stone he believed was sacred. His father had taught him to do so. His grandfather, too. But as the years passed, the ritual became dull, mechanical. His hands moved, but his heart was far away."

"One day, an old wandering monk visited his village. Observing the boy's offering, the monk asked, 'Tell me, child, who are you offering this water to?' Rivan replied flatly, 'To the stone. It is a ritual.'"

"The monk smiled and said, 'Then you are merely watering a rock. Not your soul.'"

"This shook Rivan. That night, he sat before the stone in silence. He watched the flame of the lamp flicker. He placed his hand on the cold surface of the rock. And he whispered—not a mantra, not a chant—but the truth of his heart: his longing, his fears, his dreams.

That night, he didn't perform a ritual. He opened himself."

"From that day, every act he performed—lighting the lamp, pouring the water, offering the flowers—became not something to finish, but something to feel. Not performance. Presence. His stone never moved, never spoke. But Rivan's spirit awakened."

Guruji turned back to Akshaya and said, *"To transform manifestation into a ritual of devotion, let it begin with presence. Let your list of dreams become your sacred offering. Let your affirmations rise from stillness, not urgency. Light your candle not because you must, but because you yearn to keep your inner fire alive."*

He added, "Devotion is born when we remember who we are making the offering to—not a universe outside us, but the divine listening within us."

Key Reflections:

- A manifestation practice becomes a ritual when it is done *with love*, not *for results*.

- Obligation pushes us to act from fear of consequence. Devotion pulls us to act from joy and reverence.

- Even the simplest action—writing an intention, lighting a lamp, visualising a goal—when done with emotional presence, becomes a sacred act.

As Guruji's voice softened into silence, a gentle wind stirred through Buddha Hall. The moment was still, yet alive—like a heart that prays not with words, but with being.

Akshaya closed his eyes, not in retreat, but in remembrance. And devotion, once distant, began to whisper again.

Dev asked, "What methods do we use to track our progress and celebrate small wins, and how do these practices impact our motivation?"

Guruji gently opened his eyes. A soft smile curved on his lips.

"Progress," he began, "is like the blooming of a lotus. If you wait only for the full bloom to admire it, you will miss the miracle of each unfolding petal."

He paused, letting the silence settle like dew.

"I will tell you the story of Smitha," he said, "a young woman who once joined our retreat years ago. She had come seeking clarity. But she was impatient—she wanted transformation overnight. She would meditate, then open her journal and write, 'Nothing happened today.' The next day, 'Still no change.' She judged every moment, every breath, through the lens of a final result."

"One evening, I invited her to the garden. I handed her a lantern and asked her to walk to the mango grove at the far end. It was a moonless night."

"After some time, she returned, a little flustered."

'I could only see a few steps ahead, Guruji! I didn't know if I was on the right path!'

I smiled and said, 'Yet you reached, didn't you? Because you trusted each step and the light you held was enough.'"

"We don't need to see the whole path," Guruji continued, "we only need to honour the light we carry today. And every step we take in awareness is a victory worth acknowledging."

He turned to Dev. "So how do we track progress? Not only by the final goal, but by the *integrity of our steps*. A deep breath taken during anxiety. A kind word offered when anger surged. A day without self-criticism. These are not small wins, Dev. These are soul-victories."

He added:

"Keep a **Compassionate Ledger**, not a critical one. Let your journal hold not only your struggles, but your silent triumphs—the days you rose despite resistance, the moments you chose trust over fear."

"Create **Rituals of Celebration**—not grand ones. Light a lamp. Say thank you. Offer a flower. Mark your progress with love, not just measurement."

"The heart expands," Guruji said softly, "when it is seen and honoured. Each time you acknowledge your effort, you water the roots of perseverance. Celebration is not vanity. It is nourishment."

A hush filled the hall. Dev looked down, eyes misted—not from sorrow, but from recognition.

Padma whispered, "I think I've forgotten to celebrate myself for too long…"

Astyn, her voice tender yet resolute, leaned forward and asked: "Guruji, how do we maintain dedication during periods when results seem slow or invisible, and what mindset shifts help us sustain momentum?"

Guruji gazed at her with—tenderness. He closed his eyes for a moment.

The Story of the Silent Sculptor

"There was once a sculptor in the old town of Mahabalipuram," Guruji began, "who was known not for what he created, but for what he *continued* to work on—even when no one understood why."

"He would visit the same rock every day, chiselling it in silence. For years. The townspeople mocked him. Some said he had lost his mind. Others offered him easier work. But he never explained. He would only smile and say, 'The form is speaking to me. I'm listening.'"

"Ten years passed. Ten *long* years. Then one day, he stopped. He stepped back. And there stood a **divine form of Nataraja**, so detailed that even the wrinkles on the feet seemed to breathe. The townspeople were awestruck. They asked, 'How did you keep going when the stone looked the same for so long?'"

The sculptor replied: "'Each strike of the chisel was a dialogue with destiny. I wasn't sculpting the statue. I was sculpting *myself*.'"

Guruji looked at Astyn and continued gently:

"Dedication isn't about speed. It's about *direction*."

"When we don't see immediate results, the mind panics. It equates visible progress with success. But the soul knows: growth is often **rooted, not visible**."

"A seed doesn't doubt its journey because it can't see the sun. It just keeps moving upward, *trusting in the dark*."

He paused, then offered the wisdom in layers:

- **Mindset Shift 1: Trade Urgency for Intimacy.**

    "Don't ask, 'Why is it taking so long?' Ask, 'What is this moment teaching me?' The process becomes a partner, not a problem."

- **Mindset Shift 2: Redefine Progress.**

    "Progress isn't only when the world claps. It's also when your inner critic falls silent for a day. That is monumental."

- **Mindset Shift 3: Anchor to Intention, Not Outcome.**

    "When your why is strong, the when becomes less frightening."

"When the fire of desire dims, add devotion—not more pressure."

Guruji then shared a practice:

"Each night, ask yourself: *Did I honour the dream today, even in one small way?* A single drop of effort every day carves rivers into mountains."

Astyn wiped a quiet tear. Not from pain, but from the release of carrying too much alone.

Padma whispered, "Maybe we all are sculptors… carving away the doubt, bit by bit."

Guruji nodded, "Indeed. And one day, even if the world doesn't notice… *You* will see what you've become. And it will have been worth every unseen effort."

Guruji had called for a midday break. After their delicious satvik meal, many devotees wandered toward the forest's edge, drawn by the serenity of the cascading stream. Under the shade of a massive ancient tree, they gathered—Apeksha, Nita, Lalitha, Sam, Alice, Sofia, Bhavya, Aarna, Dev, John, and Vidyarthi. A few sat quietly with their feet in the water. Others rested, their eyes half-closed in reflection.

Soon, Nita leaned closer, her voice soft, "Apeksha... the story you once shared during the winter retreat... we've never forgotten it. Will you tell it again?"

Vidyarthi added, "Yes, the one about the woman who came here in silence. It stayed with me."

Apeksha gently nodded, her voice carrying the weight of reverence.

The Woman from Bengaluru

"Many years ago," Apeksha began, "a woman named Pushpa came to this retreat. She had not spoken a word in days, not even when she registered. Her eyes were hollow, like she had forgotten how to feel joy."

"She had lost her husband unexpectedly. He was her best friend, her anchor, her home. His absence was not just a gap in her life—it was a collapse of everything she believed in. People had tried to console her with words like 'time will heal' and 'he's in a better place.' But those words only echoed louder against her silence."

Apeksha paused as a breeze swept through, lifting a few dry leaves into the air.

"She chose to attend the retreat because someone told her about Guruji... not as a spiritual teacher, but as a presence where brokenness didn't have to hide."

The Candle and the Flame

"One evening, during satsang, Guruji asked every devotee to light a small candle and sit in stillness. The light in Buddha Hall was dimmed. Each flame flickered softly. He then said, *'Let your pain sit beside you. Don't push it away. Just hold it like you'd hold a frightened child.'*

"Pushpa sat with her candle, and for the first time in months… she cried. But it wasn't the wild, collapsing grief—it was a quiet weeping. The kind that comes when the heart begins to remember it's still beating."

Apeksha's voice softened, "Later that night, she wrote in her journal— *'I thought my love died with him. But today, I felt it flicker inside me again… like this flame. Gentle. Alive. A beginning.'*"

The Transformation

"She stayed the full ten days of the retreat," Apeksha continued. "And though she didn't speak much, something changed in her. Her silence no longer felt hollow—it felt sacred. She helped in the kitchen, arranged flowers near the Jyoti, and even smiled at strangers. That final day, she bowed before Guruji with hands trembling, and said just one thing: *'You helped me remember that grief is not the absence of love—it is love, asking to be transformed.'*"

There was a deep silence in the group. The waterfall sang behind them, and birds flew across the sky in patterns only nature understood.

Alice wiped a tear. Bhavya whispered, "It's strange how someone we've never met can teach us so much."

John added, "And how brokenness, when held with grace, becomes beautiful."

Nita looked toward the flowing water. "Pushpa's story… it feels like a part of all of us."

Apeksha nodded. "That's the power of true stories. They don't belong to just one heart. They awaken something in everyone listening."

The Call of the Bell

As the orange hues of evening began to paint the sky, Kiran stretched and said gently, "The time for the next session is near." The devotees stood slowly, their hearts quieter and fuller than before.

As they walked back toward Buddha Hall, the air seemed clearer, the breeze more sacred. Some carried the weight of the story, others the lightness of healing it offered.

And somewhere in that forest, perhaps the memory of Pushpa walked with them.

CHAPTER XIII

Rule 12 – Spreading Love and Positivity

"When you give love freely, you open the floodgates for the universe to return it in abundance."

– Shree Shambav

Synopsis

Manifestation reaches its highest expression when it moves beyond self-interest into the realm of service. This chapter reveals how love and positivity are powerful forces that amplify your manifestation energy when shared with others. By consciously contributing to the well-being of your community and practising acts of kindness, you create a ripple effect that magnifies abundance and fulfilment—for yourself and the world around you.

You will explore ways to cultivate generosity, build meaningful connections, and understand how every positive action expands your energetic field. Spreading love becomes both a manifestation tool and a pathway to living a deeply meaningful life.

The fragrance of jasmine and vetiver hung gently in the air as Padma, her voice calm yet filled with inner curiosity, asked: "Guruji, how does our expression of love and kindness influence our own sense of abundance and manifestation success?"

Guruji looked at her with quiet warmth. After a pause long enough to soften every thought in the room, he began.

The River That Never Dries

"There was once a woman," Guruji said, "who lived on the edge of a drought-stricken village. Her name was Kamala. Every morning, despite her own scarcity, she filled a small pot of water from her nearly empty well and left it at the roadside for weary travellers. Some drank from it, others did not. But she kept placing it there, day after day."

"The villagers mocked her. 'You barely have enough for yourself. Why give away even a drop?' But Kamala would only smile and say, 'Water finds its way to those who trust its flow.'"

"One summer, the well went completely dry. The Earth cracked. Crops failed. The village began to panic. But on the fifth day of parching heat, something strange happened. A travelling monk arrived— parched and exhausted. Kamala, despite having no water left, brought him shade, a cool cloth, and a meal made from her last handful of grain."

"The monk, moved by her compassion, wept silently and then pointed to a mound of stones behind her hut. 'Dig there,' he said."

"They laughed at him, but Kamala believed. That evening, she and a few curious children began to dig. By morning, they struck a new spring—clear, abundant, and sweet."

"That spring never ran dry. And soon, the whole village came to draw from Kamala's well. The one who gave when she had little, now received in abundance—not just water, but reverence, peace, and joy."

Guruji turned to Padma, his voice soft as a lullaby yet sharp with truth.

"Love and kindness," he said, "are not expenses. They are investments in the unseen economy of the soul. When we give freely—not out of calculation, but out of devotion—we become open channels through which the universe flows."

"Abundance is not something we chase; it is something we become. And the more love we pour out, the more room we create within ourselves to receive."

He leaned forward slightly.

"The miser may gather, but it is the giver who glows. The river that gives water to all, never runs dry—it is fed by unseen mountains of grace."

A hushed silence followed. No one moved. Even the birds outside seemed to still themselves in reverence.

Padma's eyes shimmered. A subtle smile, more sacred than joy, dawned on her lips. She understood—not just with the mind, but with the heart.

And in that understanding, something unseen began to flow within everyone in that hall: **a quiet, unstoppable abundance.**

The stillness was gently broken when Akshatha, her voice reverent and thoughtful, asked: "Guruji, what are some meaningful ways we can contribute positively to our community or circle, and how might these acts transform our vibration?"

The Lantern in the Dark

"There was once a young man," Guruji began, "named Adarsh, who lived in a quiet village nestled in the hills. He had dreams, yes—but more than that, he carried a silent grief. He often felt unseen, unheard, as though his existence was just another stone in the long road of life. His heart longed for significance, but he didn't know where to begin."

"One evening, during a heavy monsoon, the village lost power. Darkness swallowed everything. In panic, children cried, elders stumbled, and fear took root. But Adarsh lit a small lantern outside his home and placed it on the stone wall beside the road. It was a simple gesture. He did it without any thought of reward."

"To his surprise, a few villagers began gathering around it—first the children, then the elderly, then neighbours who had never spoken much to each other. Someone brought warm rice. Another brought a flute. Conversations were shared. Laughter bloomed. That single light became a place of warmth, comfort, and connection."

"The next day, Adarsh was surprised to see others setting out lanterns of their own. It became a ritual—each person lighting a lamp not just for themselves, but for others. And with time, what began as a single act of service became a living reminder that no matter how dark the world gets, we can always be the bearer of light."

Guruji paused. The hall was still, as if the story itself had created a soft glow in the hearts of the listeners.

Then he said with gentle gravity:

"When we serve others—not from obligation, but from the overflow of our inner compassion—we rise in frequency. We align with the rhythm of the universe. Every act of kindness becomes a ripple, every offering a seed."

"You see, the river does not drink its own water. The tree does not eat its own fruit. Their purpose is fulfilled in their giving. And so it is with us. The more we contribute, the more we dissolve the walls of separation. In helping another rise, we rise."

He looked at Akshatha with affection, and added:

"You don't need wealth to serve. You need presence. A listening ear, a kind word, a shared meal, a walk with someone in grief— these are sacred acts. They may look small, but they recalibrate the energy of an entire space. They're not just good deeds… they are soul-prints."

Akshatha gently whispered, "Thank you, Guruji."

Guruji nodded, "The heart that gives, lives. The vibration of service is the vibration of the sacred. Let your contribution not be a burden, but a prayer."

Apeksha, with her palms gently folded, looked up at Guruji and asked with genuine curiosity and wonder: "Guruji, how do *we experience the ripple effect of positivity in our life, and what stories or examples illustrate this impact?"*

Guruji gave her a gentle nod, his eyes closing briefly as though touching something sacred within. Then, with a breath that carried both memory and presence, he began to speak.

The Ripple at Shantivan

"There was a woman named Uma," he began, "who once attended a retreat at Shantivan, a place not so different from here. She was grieving—a quiet sorrow that had folded her spirit inward after losing her partner. She hardly spoke during the retreat. She sat alone, at meals, at satsangs, walking always a step behind the group."

"One afternoon, after a contemplative session, she was sitting by the edge of the lotus pond, tears rolling silently. A young man named Ravi, another seeker on the path, noticed her and simply sat beside her—not to fix, not to speak, but just to *be*. After a while, he offered her a cup of warm Tulsi tea and smiled."

"That one moment of silent compassion changed something in her."

"She later told me that it was not his words, but his presence that reminded her she was not alone. In the following days, she began smiling. Then slowly talking.

Then laughing. And by the end of the retreat, she was the one offering tea to another newcomer who had arrived with silent pain."

"That spark Ravi shared passed on. And the one Uma shared passed further. A cascade. One act became the root of many blooms."

Guruji opened his eyes, looking gently at Apeksha.

"This," he said, "is the ripple effect of positivity."

"It rarely shouts. It doesn't seek recognition. But like a pebble dropped into a still pond, its waves travel far beyond the eye. A kind word spoken with presence, a gesture made without agenda, a truth shared from the heart—they echo across hearts, lives, even generations."

The Mirror and the Mountain

"Imagine," Guruji continued, "that you are standing in front of a mountain and you shout 'I love you!' What do you hear back?"

Apeksha smiled, "The echo… 'I love you.'"

He nodded.

"Life echoes our vibration. If we radiate gratitude, compassion, hope, it doesn't just end with us—it reflects, magnifies, returns. And touches others long after we've left the space."

Real Ripples, Subtle Shifts

"There are schoolteachers," he said softly, "who simply *believed* in a child who no one else did—and that belief became the seed of a life that flourished. There are nurses who held a patient's hand when they had no family, and that presence became the medicine. These ripples may never be written in books, but they are etched into souls."

"You see, Apeksha," he said, "each of us is a thread. And the way we move, think, give, love—we shape the entire tapestry. You are never just doing something 'for someone.' You're doing it *through* them—for all those they will meet after."

"What you radiate—be it bitterness or kindness—is never just yours. It becomes part of the collective breath."

Apeksha's eyes welled slightly, not with sorrow, but with reverence.

She whispered, "Thank you, Guruji… I understand now."

Guruji smiled.

"Be the pebble that chooses kindness. Even if you never see the shore it touches, trust the wave it sends."

Akshaya asked, "Guruji, in what ways can shifting focus from self-centered desires to collective well-being deepen our manifestation practice?"

Guruji nodded slowly, eyes bright with knowing, and began.

The Story of the Lamp Lighter

"Many years ago," Guruji began, "in a small coastal village in Tamil Nadu, there lived a man named Madhavan. He was a poor oil vendor who made a modest living filling small brass lamps in the homes of the village. He had a quiet dream—to become wealthy, to own land, and to have a better life for himself. Every morning, he prayed for abundance."

"But year after year, little changed. The oil cans grew heavier, the coins fewer. One day, an old mendicant stopped him and asked for oil for his temple lamp. Irritated but unable to refuse, Madhavan poured a few drops."

'You give as if the oil will run out,' the sage said, 'but light only grows when shared.'

"These words stayed with Madhavan. That evening, for the first time, he lit a lamp not in his own house, but outside the village well—so that others drawing water at night might have light."

"Something shifted."

"Every evening thereafter, he placed one more lamp—outside the school, near the temple steps, by the fisherman's dock. People began noticing. Some thanked him. Some brought their own lamps. Light spread—not just in the village, but within him."

"He began receiving more work—not because he asked, but because people trusted him. Slowly, his fortune changed. But more importantly, so did his heart. The wealth he had long sought for himself, came when he *became* the source of light for others."

Beyond the Mirror

Guruji paused and continued softly, "Most people approach manifestation like looking into a mirror—'Give me this, bring me that.' But the universe is not a mirror. It is more like fertile soil. If you plant seeds that only feed you, your harvest will be limited. But if your seeds feed many, the soil will feed you back a hundredfold."

"The shift from *me* to *we* doesn't dilute your power—it multiplies it."

Desire as Offering

"Akshaya," Guruji said, turning toward her, "when you set an intention, ask yourself, 'How does this serve the whole?' Even if your desire is personal—a home, a job, a healing—imagine how it can ripple outwards."

"A healed you heals others. A peaceful you brings calm to your family. A fulfilled you gives generously."

"When desire becomes offering, the universe receives it with reverence. You are no longer begging at the door—you are building the temple."

The Shift of the Sun

"Do you know," Guruji asked, "why life on Earth exists at all?"

Akshaya shook his head gently.

"Because the sun gives without asking."

"It does not choose which flower to feed, which tree to bless. Its only dharma is to shine. And in doing so, it sustains life."

"You too, have that sun within you."

"When you turn your manifestation from acquisition to contribution, from craving to creating—you begin to shine from that place. And life arranges itself not just *for* you, but *through* you."

The Hall Was Silent. Full. Whole.

Tears welled in Akshaya's eyes. Not from sadness, but from the quiet realisation of something vast and tender.

Guruji smiled, his voice like the rustling of the Bodhi leaves outside.

"The highest manifestation is not what you take—but what you awaken in others."

Final Chapter

The Magnetic Life

"When your soul's mission aligns with your daily actions, you become an unstoppable force of attraction."

– Shree Shambav

Synopsis

The journey through these rules culminates in becoming a living embodiment of the Law of Attraction—a magnetic life where your thoughts, emotions, and actions align effortlessly with your highest soul mission. This epilogue invites you to see your manifestation practice not merely as a tool for personal gain but as a sacred path of service, growth, and deeper connection to the universe.

Here, reflection becomes a powerful ritual, helping you integrate what you've learned and step fully into your role as a radiant example of conscious creation. Embracing this magnetic life means inspiring others through your authenticity and allowing your soul's purpose to unfold naturally in the world.

After a long, soul-filled silence, Guruji slowly rose from his asana.

His presence lingered like incense in the air—silent, weightless, and reverent. Without a word, he bowed gently toward the altar flame, then toward the circle of his gathered disciples. His departure from the Buddha Hall was not abrupt, but ceremonial—like the closing of a sacred scripture after the last verse has been heard not just with the ears, but with the heart.

It marked the end of the day's session—and the retreat itself.

One by one, the devotees followed in a quiet procession, as if reluctant to disturb the stillness that now enveloped the hall. Outside, Kumbhariyur had draped itself in the night's velvet shawl. The sky was aglow with starlight, each star like a soft whisper from the heavens, reminding them of the infinite. A gentle breeze carried the scent of jasmine, sandalwood, and the sweet smoke from the retreat's final oil lamp.

After their humble dinner—served in silence and received with reverence—the seekers gathered around the fire beneath the open sky.

The flames flickered and danced, casting golden reflections in their eyes, mirroring the quiet illumination that had begun to stir within.

The atmosphere was hushed but intimate—voices low, laughter tender, as they began to reflect on the day's teachings. The fire became more than warmth; it became witness—crackling softly as if listening.

They didn't just discuss Guruji's words.

They carried them.

Like seeds beneath their ribs.

Sam broke the silence gently; his voice tinged with wonder and reflection.

"Nita, how has your understanding of the Law of Attraction evolved through this journey, and in what ways do you feel ready to embody it fully?"

Nita didn't answer right away. She stared into the fire, her fingers gently wrapped around her tea. The embers sparked memories, insights, and moments of surrender. After a few heartbeats, she spoke—softly, yet with a clarity that silenced even the wind.

"I used to think the Law of Attraction was about wanting," Nita said.

"About writing affirmations and thinking positive, about vision boards and lists of desires—like giving the universe my wishlist and waiting for delivery."

The group chuckled gently. It was a familiar beginning for many.

"But something shifted here," she continued, her voice deepening.

"Especially in those moments of silence… during the walking meditations, and especially during that story Guruji shared about the potter by the river."

The Inner Garden

"It's like… before, I was trying to plant trees by throwing seeds into the sky. Hoping they'd land somewhere fertile. But now, I realise the soil was always within me."

Her eyes lifted toward the fireflies dancing beyond the firelight.

"The Law of Attraction is not just about pulling things *toward* us. It's about becoming the kind of space where those things can belong."

"It's less about attracting and more about *aligning*."

The Tapestry of Trust

"I learned that life doesn't always give us what we want—but it always gives us what we're ready to receive. When we stop chasing and start listening, our desires deepen. They become less noisy… more sacred."

She paused, gazing toward the Banyan tree in the distance.

"Now, I don't ask the universe to change for me. I ask to change in such a way that I become ready for what the universe is already offering."

The Fire Within

The fire crackled louder now, as if echoing her words.

"This retreat taught me that manifestation is not just about getting. It's about giving birth—to new versions of ourselves. It's about dissolving the old patterns, releasing the noise, and aligning with the rhythm of grace."

Her eyes shimmered, reflecting both firelight and conviction.

"I feel ready now… not to make life bend to my will, but to let my will dance with life."

There was a long, sacred silence after she finished.

Even the fire seemed to settle into stillness.

Aastha reached out, holding Nita's hand. Sam nodded deeply. Kiran, who rarely showed emotion, exhaled a quiet, heartfelt *"thank you."*

The Law of Attraction had moved from concept to communion.

No longer a tool for wish-making.

But a path of becoming.

The fire crackled gently, its orange glow mirrored in their eyes. Beyond the firelight, the Kumbhariyur sky stretched vast and black, adorned with a thousand watchful stars. The wind carried a sacred hush—as if the universe itself had leaned in to listen.

Lalitha, her voice soft but certain, broke the silence.

"Rohith… What is your broader soul mission? And how can your manifestation practice serve that greater purpose?"

A silence followed. Not empty—but full. The kind of silence that feels like a doorway opening within.

Rohith didn't answer right away. He looked into the flames, as if searching for words hidden in the dancing embers. His breath slowed. A deep inhale… and then a pause. His voice, when it came, carried the texture of memory, of inner ache, of awakening.

"For a long time," he began, "I thought my purpose was achievement. Success. To build something great. To leave a legacy. And so I chased. Titles. Trophies. The illusion of being 'seen.' And yet… I always felt unseen by the one who mattered most—myself."

He glanced up at the stars.

"It wasn't until life broke me open—until I lost what I thought defined me—that I began to hear a different voice inside. Not the one that said, 'Become something,' but the one that whispered, 'Remember who you already are.'"

He folded his hands loosely in his lap, like one holding a prayer.

"My soul mission," he said gently, "is to heal. To hold space for others who have forgotten their worth. To remind people—quietly, gently—that they were never broken, only buried beneath noise and hurt and fear."

"Manifestation, for me now, is no longer a tool to get. It's a path to give. I manifest inner stillness so I can offer it to those in chaos. I manifest love so I can be a vessel of it in rooms where love has gone missing."

He paused, eyes glistening but steady.

"The oak tree does not grow tall to be admired. It grows because its roots hunger for depth. And in doing so, it shelters birds,

cools weary travellers, and stands as a silent witness to storms and seasons."

"I don't wish to manifest a throne. I wish to become the soil in which others remember how to rise."

The fire cracked again—louder this time—as if affirming his words. The group sat in reverent silence. No one rushed to speak. Because sometimes, the soul doesn't need a reply. It only needs to be witnessed.

Lalitha whispered, her voice carrying the softness of morning dew, **"You're already walking it, Rohith."**

And somewhere beyond the fire, the night exhaled—peacefully.

Apeksha's voice carried across the hush with gentleness but sincerity.

"Kieron, how can you continue to nurture your magnetic energy daily, becoming a beacon for others on their path?"

The question lingered in the space like sacred incense. The group grew still. Even the wind seemed to pause.

Kieron closed his eyes for a moment. Not in retreat, but in listening. His hands, clasped together, trembled slightly—not out of nervousness, but reverence for the truth he was about to share.

"There was a time," he began softly, "when I confused magnetic energy with charisma. I thought if I could speak well, dress right, or gather followers, I would become someone worth looking up to."

He opened his eyes and looked into the flames, their light reflecting in his irises like tiny suns.

"But I was wrong. That kind of energy draws eyes, not hearts. It creates echo chambers, not true impact."

The group leaned in. Not physically—but with attention, with presence.

"True magnetism, I've learned," he continued, "comes not from performing light—but becoming it."

He paused, then turned to Apeksha.

"You asked how I nurture that each day?" he smiled. "It's not in grand acts, but quiet devotion."

"Every morning, before the world rushes in, I sit with myself—not to judge, but to witness. I speak to my fears like they are children. I forgive yesterday. I thank the breath. And I ask a simple question: 'How can I be of use today—not to impress, but to uplift?'"

"It's in the way I speak to the man who delivers my groceries. In how I listen to someone without planning my reply. It's in how I choose content that feeds my soul—not just my ambition."

He looked up at the moon.

"We often try to shine like the sun—loud, glorious, visible. But I want to be like the moon. Quiet. Reflective. Drawing tides, influencing hearts—not by blinding, but by being."

He turned toward the group, his voice a whisper, but his presence vast.

"If I can walk each day with integrity… if I can respond with love when it's hardest… if I can make even one person feel seen without needing anything in return… then that is magnetism. That is the beacon I want to become—not one that says, 'Follow me,' but one that whispers, 'Come home to yourself.'"

A hush settled.

Roopa clutched her shawl closer. Vasudeva stared at the fire with misted eyes. Padma softly whispered, "That was… real."

Apeksha simply smiled and placed her hand on Kieron's shoulder.

"Thank you," she said, **"for reminding us what it truly means to radiate."**

And under the canopy of stars, it felt as though a hundred invisible lamps had been lit—not around them, but within.

Padma leaned forward slightly, her eyes kind but penetrating. "Akshatha," she said, "what intentions or commitments are you ready to make to honour your role as a conscious creator in the world?"

The question didn't fall—it landed. Gently. Powerfully. Like the drop of rain that touches the parched earth and awakens something beneath the surface.

Akshatha looked up. Her fingers brushed the edge of her shawl, her breath slow, steady. The firelight danced in her eyes as she stared not into the flame—but beyond it, into something only she could see.

"There was a time," she began softly, "when I believed that life was something that happened to me. That I was a passenger—on the waves of others' decisions, the winds of fate, the storms of circumstance."

Her voice trembled, not with fear, but with memory.

"I used to pray only when I was afraid. Create only when I was broken. Give only when I had something left over."

She glanced toward the night sky, where the stars blinked like ancient messengers.

"But something shifted when I came to Kumbhariyur. When I sat before Guruji. When I watched how even silence here speaks."

She turned to Padma, her voice clearer now, fuller.

"I saw that to be a conscious creator is not to control life—but to enter into a relationship with it. It is to wake up each morning not asking, 'What can I get?' but 'What am I meant to *give* today—with presence, with integrity, with love?'"

"So my first intention," she continued, her words deliberate, "is to treat each thought as a seed. To not plant out of fear, scarcity, or ego. But from the truth. From the vision I hold not only for myself, but for the world I wish to help shape."

"My second commitment," she said, placing a hand on her heart, "is to not wait for perfect conditions to begin. The world does not need my perfection—it needs my participation. My voice. My flawed, evolving, trembling-but-true self."

"And lastly," she breathed in deeply, "I commit to loving without calculation. To forgive faster. To risk showing up even when I am unsure. Because I've seen now… that we are all artists—painting the world not with brushes, but with the energy we carry."

A stillness fell over the circle.

Even the wind slowed down—as if listening.

Bhavya wiped away a quiet tear. Kiran closed his eyes in acknowledgement. Vasudeva whispered, "That is devotion."

Padma leaned in, touched Akshatha's hand gently, and said, **"You're not just ready. You already are."**

And at that moment, Akshatha wasn't just speaking about her commitments—She *was* her commitment.

A silent shift had occurred. A thread of consciousness had been sewn tighter into the fabric of the universe.

And somewhere in the distance, a lone bird sang—not as an ending, but as a blessing.

The night in Kumbhariyur lingered like an old melody—soft, unhurried, echoing between the trees and hearts. The stars above shimmered like ancient witnesses, and the embers in the fire pit pulsed with a gentle glow, as if reluctant to fade. Around it sat those who had shared not just meals and moments—but awakenings.

They weren't merely devotees anymore. Something unspoken had woven them together into seekers, mirrors, and gentle witnesses of each other's becoming.

Sofia looked around—the soft faces warmed by the firelight, the eyes that now held deeper stillness. With a voice half-whisper, half-wish, she said,

"We all have to meet again. At the next retreat."

Her words didn't need explanation.

It wasn't just about a gathering.

It was about remembering.

It was about choosing not to forget the versions of themselves they had uncovered here—the raw, luminous, unmasked selves.

Kiran gave a small nod, the kind that speaks of sacred agreements. *"Yes," he said, "because the world outside will try to put us back in boxes we've outgrown. We need to return… not to escape life, but to remember how to meet it."*

Bhavya stirred the fire absently and added, "Coming here felt like peeling off old skins. I don't want to lose what I've uncovered."

John, who had spoken least during the retreat, said softly, "In the silence here, I met a part of me I didn't know how to hear back home."

He looked at Sofia. "We owe it to ourselves to come back. Not just to this place—but to this presence."

Akshaya, watching the glowing coals, drew a slow breath.
"This isn't just a place," he said. "It's a mirror. The way the air breathes. The way Guruji pauses before answering. The way each of us held space for the other's truth."

He looked around the circle.

"Let's carry this with us—not as memory, but as practice."

The fire cracked gently, its sparks flying up like stars trying to return home.

No one rushed to leave. No one broke the silence too soon.

Each of them knew that life, with its noise and demands, was waiting just beyond the mountain's bend. But tonight… tonight was a vow.

A vow not made by shouting promises into the air, but by the weight of still eyes meeting. By the quiet nods. By the touch of hands on shoulders.

Sofia looked up at the stars.

"May we never forget," she said. **"And may we always return—not just here, but to the truth within us."**

And as the fire dimmed and the night deepened, it was clear:

The retreat was ending…

But the journey into truth had just begun.

Epilogue

By now, you've travelled through the quiet corridors of your mind, the radiant chambers of your heart, and the hidden valleys of your soul. You've looked deeply—not just outward toward your desires, but inward, toward the one who desires. You've learned to listen not only to the loudness of the world, but to the subtle pulse of your own being.

And maybe—just maybe—you've come to see that the Law of Attraction is not a secret formula, but a sacred mirror.

It reflects who you are becoming, not only what you are asking for.

It doesn't simply answer your wishes—it aligns your *essence* with your *existence*.

We often believe that power lies in effort—grasping, striving, chasing.

But magnetism lies in *truth*.

And the most magnetic force in the universe is not control, but coherence—when your thoughts, emotions, beliefs, and actions sing in harmony.

This is the magnetic life.

What It Means to Live a Magnetic Life

To live magnetically is to walk with inner clarity, even when the path is fogged.

It is to feel your emotions fully, but not be ruled by them.

It is to act not from fear or proving, but from faith and alignment.

It is to welcome the unfolding—not as punishment or reward, but as a reflection of your current vibration and a teacher for your next becoming.

A magnetic life is a gentle life. Not passive, but present. Not perfect, but purposeful.

You still fall. You still feel doubt. But you meet yourself now—with softness, with wisdom, with deep self-regard.

You stop begging life to prove your worth—and instead, begin radiating from it.

You no longer chase love, success, peace…

You *become* them.

A Final Whisper

So pause now.

Take a breath—not to rush forward, but to let this all sink in.

You are no longer who you were at the start of this book. You carry something new now—not because the world has changed, but because you have returned to the part of you that *always knew*.

Your soul did not come here to survive on crumbs of manifestation.

It came to remember its wholeness—and create from there.

So live with clarity.

Feel with truth.

Act with intention.

Rest in trust.

And when doubt returns—as it will—place your hand on your heart and say:

"I am here. I am aligned. I am becoming."

"What I seek is already seeking me."

"I attract what I am ready to receive."

Because you are no longer chasing the magnetic life. You are already living it.

Closing Invitation:

Before you step into your next creation, take a quiet moment with yourself. Light a candle, close your eyes, and say aloud or silently:

"I welcome my future not as a stranger to be impressed,

But as a friend I already know.

I walk in clarity, emotion, and action—

And I trust the unseen to carry what I am ready to receive."

Now, go.

Live it.

Be it.

Attract it.

APPENDICES

APPENDICES A

Living the Magnetic Life

Practice and Reflection

Reader Reflection Journal Prompt

"Becoming the Vibration You Seek"

Take time with this prompt. Light a candle. Sit somewhere still. Let your breath deepen and your body soften. Then reflect on the following:

1. Who have I become through this journey?

What inner shifts have occurred in the way I think, feel, believe, or act?

2. What are three beliefs I now hold that feel empowering and true?

How do these beliefs affect how I see the world and what I expect from life?

3. What desire or dream now feels possible that once felt distant?

How can I nurture this vision with emotional alignment and action?

4. When I imagine my highest self—calm, clear, radiant—what does that version of me say, do, and believe?

How can I begin showing up as that version today?

5. What daily rituals, thoughts, or emotional shifts keep me in harmony with my desires?

What drains my energy or pulls me out of alignment?

6. What does "success" now mean to me—not by society's terms, but by my soul's?

7. What am I willing to release in order to receive what I've asked for?

8. Finish this sentence:

"My life is a magnetic force because I choose to…"

Daily Manifestation Ritual

"Align, Attract, Allow" – A 10-Minute Morning Practice

This ritual can be done in the morning or at any quiet time. The purpose is to energetically align your thoughts, emotions, and actions to your intention—bringing the Law of Attraction into conscious, loving practice.

1. Ground (1 minute)

Sit still. Feel your body. Place your hand on your heart or belly. Inhale slowly for 4 counts, exhale for 6. Do this three times. Let your body soften and your awareness return home.

Affirm silently:

"I am safe in this moment. I am present in this breath."

2. Set Your Intention (2 minutes)

Ask yourself:

"What energy do I choose to embody today?"
Is it love? Confidence? Peace? Joy? Focus? Gratitude?

Visualise yourself living today from that energy. See yourself smiling, creating, receiving, giving. Feel it fully. Let it wash through you.

Affirm aloud:

"Today, I align with the energy of _____. I move through the world as a living expression of it."

3. Speak Your Manifestation (2 minutes)

Choose one clear desire. Say it aloud in the present tense with deep emotion. For example:

"I am attracting opportunities that honour my truth and purpose."
"I feel deeply supported in my finances, health, and relationships."
"I am living my dream life with ease and joy."

Repeat your desire slowly, three times. Feel it. Smile. Trust.

4. Offer Gratitude (2 minutes)

Write or whisper at least three things you're grateful for, especially things you've already manifested or that are on their way.

Example:

- "I'm grateful for the chance to begin again today."
- "I'm grateful for my creative ideas and courage."
- "I'm grateful for the support I feel, seen or unseen."

5. Release and Trust (2 minutes)

Close your eyes. Picture your desire floating gently into the sky like a paper lantern. Let it rise. Let it go.

Say silently or aloud:

"I let go with love. I trust the timing. I am aligned with all I need."

Breathe in. Smile softly. You've done enough.

Closing Blessing

"May your thoughts be clear,

Your emotions are pure,

Your actions inspired,

And your soul forever aligned

With the life that longs to meet you."

Life Coach and Philanthropist

Shree Shambav is the visionary founder of the Shree Shambav Ayur Rakshita Foundation (www.shambav-ayurrakshita.org). He founded this institution with a lofty goal: to recognise human identity across gender, ethnicity, and nationality. Through this organisation, he wants to assist all communities in realising their full potential and the intrinsic beauty of life.

Shree Shambav, a Life Coach, is dedicated to supporting people on their journeys of self-discovery and empowerment. He assists people in discovering who they are, determining what inspires and drives them, and overcoming limiting ideas. His approach clarifies what one wants in life, assisting people through goal-setting and a step-by-step process for achieving them. He empowers people to make deliberate and responsible decisions, allowing them to identify their blind spots and evolve as individuals via the use of numerous strategies and tools.

The foundation's bold, uncompromising, and compassionate ventures are always aimed at initiating the "Inner Transformation" process. They focus on spiritual growth, personal growth, and self-healing while emphasising that true progress lies in "Inclusive Growth and Co-existence." This philosophy drives all their initiatives, encouraging a holistic approach to development and well-being.

Under Shree Shambav's leadership, the foundation has launched several impactful movements:

Shree Shambav Green Movement: This mission is to create a healthy, green, and clean earth through responsible water conservation and greening initiatives. The movement strives to make the world a green paradise by encouraging sustainable living and environmental responsibility.

Shree Shambav Vidya Vedhika (Vizhuthugal): This project aims to help students and children by offering training, books, stationery, and uniforms. It aims to provide the next generation with the tools and resources they need to excel both academically and personally.

Shree Shambav and his foundation exemplify the spirit of compassion, transformation, and inclusive growth via their work, which has a profound impact on individuals and communities around the world. His work exemplifies the power of acknowledging and nourishing the human spirit, creating a world in which everyone can reach their full potential and appreciate the beauty of life.

TESTIMONIALS

Journey of Soul - Karma - "We die in our twenties and are buried at eighty." Remember that nothing can stop someone who refuses to be stopped. "Most people do not fail; they simply give up." Shree Shambav deserves full credit. It allowed me to sit and consider what I might miss out on in life. The author has delved into every aspect of our daily lives. How can a seemingly insignificant change in these seemingly insignificant details bring us such joy? The Soul of Journey teaches you the "art of living" as well as the "art of dying."

Twenty + One Series - The rich cultural heritage offered a host in twenty + one short stories with incredible imagination, morals and values prevalent at a given time, influencing how people respond to a crisis or any situation. The author has recreated images with universal values and morals. The plentiful of fascinating from faraway lands would leave the modern play and story writers a cringe. The book supports trust and immeasurable values instilling hope for the new generations.

Death - "Shree Shambav's 'Death - Light of Life and the Shadow of Death' is an extraordinary masterpiece that delves deep into the profound questions surrounding our existence and mortality. The book's opening statement, 'Nothing ever truly dies; it simply ceases to exist in one form before resuming it in another,' sets the stage for a thought-provoking exploration of death's multifaceted nature. Shambav's remarkable ability to navigate the philosophical complexities of death and our universal fear of it is both enlightening and comforting. This book is a testament to the power of understanding and acceptance."

Whispers of Eternity - "Reading 'Whispers of Eternity' by Shree Shambav was a transformative experience that left me captivated from beginning to end. Each section of this exquisite collection delves into the myriad facets of existence, offering poignant reflections on life, death, and everything in between. Shree Shambav's verses are a testament to the beauty of language and the power of expression, inviting readers to embark on a journey of self-discovery and spiritual awakening. Whether celebrating life's simple joys or grappling with the complexities of human emotion, this book is a timeless companion that speaks to the heart and soul of every reader."

Life Changing Journey Series - "Life Changing Journey Series II Inspirational Quotes" is a remarkable collection that illuminates the path to self-discovery and personal growth. With its inspiring quotes and insightful reflections, this book serves as a beacon of light in a world often shrouded in darkness. Each quote offers wisdom, guidance, and encouragement, reminding readers of their inner strength and resilience. A must-read for anyone seeking inspiration and enlightenment.

Learn To Love Yourself – "A Heartfelt Guide to Authentic Self-Love." "Learn to Love Yourself" invites readers on a transformative journey to embrace their true essence in a world often focused on external validation. Through ten insightful chapters, it gently reveals principles of genuine self-love, guiding readers to deepen their connection with themselves. Beyond surface positivity, it encourages the cultivation of resilient self-acceptance, from embracing one's unique qualities to setting empowering boundaries. With inspiring stories and practical wisdom, this book is a trusted companion on the path to inner peace, fulfilment, and joy, helping readers build lives that reflect their authentic selves.

The Power of Letting Go – This book has been a gift to my spiritual journey. Shree Shambav's insights into attachment, personal growth cycles, and forgiveness are enlightening. The concept of seven-year cycles resonated with me, helping me understand the natural phases of life. I feel more empowered to let go of what no longer serves me and step into a life of freedom and fulfilment. A truly beautiful read!

A Journey of Lasting Peace – "A Journey of Lasting Peace" feels like a trusted friend guiding you through the maze of self-discovery. The 18 transformative principles are both practical and deeply resonant, addressing everything from gratitude practices to the art of letting go. Each chapter is infused with warmth and wisdom, making it easy to apply the concepts to my life. I particularly appreciated the emphasis on physical health's connection to mental well-being; it served as a wake-up call for me to prioritise my health. This book is an invaluable resource for anyone serious about personal growth!

Astrology Unveiled Series – "Profound, Logical, and Inspiring". What stands out in Astrology Unveiled is the author's dedication to making Vedic astrology logical and approachable. Each concept flows naturally into the next, backed by examples and exercises. The insights into karma and life cycles add a philosophical depth rarely seen in astrology books. Perfect for anyone seeking spiritual growth alongside astrological knowledge!

The Entitlement Trap - "Thought-Provoking and Challenging" The book challenges readers to confront their own sense of entitlement, and that's not easy—but it's essential. The Entitlement Trap doesn't offer a one-size-fits-all approach. Instead, it's a thoughtful, layered examination of how entitlement can limit our growth. The chapter on "Defining Your Own Hill" was particularly impactful, as it pushed me to reconsider which challenges are truly worth pursuing. A thought-provoking read for those willing to do the inner work to create a life they can be proud of.

Whispers of a Dying Soul – "A Soul-Stirring Reflection on Life's Unspoken Truths" - *Whispers of a Dying Soul: Unspoken Regrets and Unlived Dreams"* is a deeply moving exploration of the unexpressed emotions and unfulfilled aspirations that shape our lives in ways we often don't realise. This book invites readers to confront the powerful, often hidden impact of regret while guiding them through a journey of introspection and healing. Each page opens a space to reflect on the choices that define us—from moments of unspoken love to neglected passions—offering a gentle reminder to live authentically and courageously.

Whispers of the Soul: A Journey Through Haiku - is a mesmerising collection that speaks directly to the heart. Each haiku is a delicate brushstroke capturing life's fleeting beauty and timeless wisdom, inviting readers into moments of deep reflection and peace. This book is a balm for the soul, guiding us to find meaning in stillness and connection in simplicity. The themes of nature, love, and mindfulness echo universal truths, resonating with quiet, powerful grace.

It's a book to be savoured slowly, cherished deeply, and returned to often. Truly, a gift for anyone seeking calm and clarity in life's chaos.

Whispers of Silence - Unlocking Inner Power through Stillness by Shree Shambav is a rare gem that beckons readers to pause, reflect, and reconnect with their inner selves. In a world that never stops talking, this book offers a profound exploration of silence—not as a void but as a rich and transformative space.

From the first page, Shree Shambav's writing resonates deeply, blending scientific insights with spiritual wisdom in a way that feels both universal and deeply personal. The author's ability to bridge the tangible and the transcendent makes this book an invaluable guide for anyone navigating the chaos of modern life.

The Power of Words: Transforming Speech, Transforming Lives - "The Power of Words is a profound and enlightening guide that has transformed the way I approach communication. Shree Shambav masterfully uncovers the hidden influence of our words on relationships, self-perception, and overall well-being. This book doesn't just teach you how to speak; it inspires mindful communication that fosters connection and trust. The insights on replacing negative patterns like gossip and judgment with kindness and authenticity are truly life-changing. The practical strategies and engaging narratives make it an invaluable resource for personal and professional growth. A must-read for anyone striving to communicate with intention, clarity, and compassion. Highly recommended!"

The Art of Intentional Living: Minimalism for a Life of Purpose - "The Art of Intentional Living is a refreshing guide to finding clarity in a cluttered world. With practical wisdom and profound insights, it inspires you to simplify, prioritise, and live with purpose. A must-read for anyone seeking balance and fulfilment."

Awakening the Infinite: The Power of Consciousness in Transforming Life - "Awakening the Infinite is a transformative guide that expands the mind and nourishes the soul. With profound insights and practical wisdom, this book beautifully explores the power of consciousness, helping readers connect with their true purpose and inner potential. It is a journey of self-discovery, healing, and spiritual awakening, offering clarity and inspiration at every turn. A must-read for anyone looking to live with greater awareness, meaning, and authenticity."

Beyond the Veil: A Journey Through Life After Death:

"This book touched me in ways few others have—it's not just about death, but about life, meaning, and the vast unknown that connects them. Beyond the Veil offers a graceful blend of science and spirit, inviting us to explore the mystery with awe rather than fear. The stories, insights, and reflections linger in your heart long after the final page. A truly transformative read that brings light on the shadows of mortality. It reminded me that in embracing death, we truly learn how to live."

Bonds Beyond Blood:

"A profoundly moving story that reminds us family is not defined by blood, but by love, sacrifice, and the courage to heal. Every chapter touched my soul with its emotional truth and timeless wisdom. Through joy, grief, and redemption, this book captures the raw beauty of human connection. I saw reflections of my own family in its pages—both the pain and the hope. A powerful, unforgettable read that lingers long after the final word."

A Journey into Spiritual Maturity: 12 Golden Rules for Inner Transformation

"This book is a gentle yet powerful guide that awakened a deeper sense of purpose within me. Each golden rule felt like a mirror reflecting truths I needed to embrace. Shree Shambav's wisdom is timeless, poetic, and profoundly grounding. It's not just a read—it's a journey into the heart of who you truly are. A must-read for anyone seeking lasting peace, clarity, and inner transformation."

The Inner Battlefield: Overcoming the Enemies of the Mind and Soul:

"This book is a powerful revelation—an honest mirror to the battles we fight within. Every chapter is a step closer to clarity, peace, and emotional mastery. Shree Shambav brilliantly transforms ancient wisdom into practical guidance for modern souls. It awakened in me a new strength to face my fears and rise above inner turmoil. A must-read for anyone seeking true inner victory and lasting transformation."

The Seeker's Gold – Unlocking Life's Greatest Treasure

The Seeker's Gold is a soul-stirring masterpiece that goes far beyond the pursuit of wealth—it is a journey into the heart of what truly matters. Each chapter unfolds with poetic wisdom and emotional depth, revealing that life's real treasure is not found in riches but in the transformation of the self. As the protagonist evolves through trials, love, and profound realisations, so does the reader. This book is a mirror for every dreamer, a lantern for every seeker, and a companion for anyone walking the path of purpose. A timeless tale that stays with you long after the final page.

Born to Rise Series I & II:

Born to Rise – Series I & II is a profound awakening—a journey that begins in silence and leads you to the core of your true power.

Series I reshapes your understanding of success, showing that clarity is more valuable than applause, and authenticity more powerful than performance.

Series II takes you deeper, unlocking the mindset and inner strategy behind meaningful, lasting growth—not just in wealth, but in wisdom.

Together, these books are not just guides—they are soul mirrors, revealing the truths you've forgotten and the strength you've always held.

This is more than reading—it's remembering who you are, and rising with purpose, not pressure.

ACKNOWLEDGEMENTS

To my grandfathers, grandmothers, mothers, fathers, aunts, uncles, neighbours, sisters, brothers, friends, and teachers, they poured in endless moral stories, retellings of Ramayana, Mahabharata, Puranas, Upanishads, and so on.

My teachers, neighbours, and kindred souls. Who provided us with a stage to perform wonderful Puranic stories and were gracious enough to acknowledge our efforts.

The artists and translators of epics have served as a source of inspiration, invigorating our spirits, making these works accessible, and enabling us to grasp the profound depths and deeper dimensions they contain.

I also cherish the stimulating conversations; I had with my wonderful mothers, Punitha Muniswamy and Uma Devi.

Our family's youngest member, Aadhya, who always overwhelmed me with questions, inspired this book.

I would likewise prefer to express gratitude to Mr Sivakumar, Mrs Roopa Sivakumar, Mr Akshaya Rajesh, Ms Akshatha Rajesh, Ms Apeksha Prabhu, Mr Akanksh Prabhu, Mr Nikash Sarasambi, and Mrs Spoorthi Nikash for their valuable inputs.

I must thank Mr Rajesh, Mr Savan Prabhu, Mrs Revathi Rajesh, Mrs Rajani Sarasambi, and Mrs Manju Reshma, who encouraged me and often suggested writing a book. Their unwavering belief that I had something valuable to offer kept me going during my writing sessions.

Love you all,

Shree Shambav

www.shambav.org

shreeshambav@gmail.com

Made in the USA
Monee, IL
03 May 2026

49438751R00194